CW00539545

MORE PRAISE FOR LABCRAFT

"Never has a craft held such promise. With gentle audacity, this book changes everything we thought we knew about change. A candid, brave, tantalizing insight into what deserves to be the defining skill set of our age. The world looks different now. So too do our prospects for change."

- Jonathan Robison, author, entrepreneur, and co-founder of Impact Hub, United Kingdom

"Labcraft is an extremely timely contribution to the movement of social innovation labs. Both reflective and practical, this important book is a must-read for anyone wishing to engage in the art and craft of generating societal change. Highly recommended."

- Christian Bason, Director, MindLab, Denmark

"An insightful and delightful voyage through a wonderful mix of stories and practical insights that can help anyone on the quest of new thinking for a better world."

- Louise Marra, Executive Director, Auckland Policy Office, New Zealand Government

"Across the world, we're seeing an explosion of interest in social and public innovation labs in all shapes and sizes. Running them well is much more a craft than a science, which is why it's so good to see serious practitioners here sharing experience and ideas—to help others achieve more hits and fewer misses".

- Geoff Mulgan, Chief Executive, Nesta, United Kingdom

"A 'lab report' about labs, Labcraft is an optimistic account and an invitation to explore the world of social labs, loaded with inspiring stories collectively written by a group of lab practitioners from around the world."

- Eduardo Staszowski, Director, Parsons DESIS Lab at The New School, New York

"Practical, sensible and yet unwaveringly inspiring. This great little collaborative book delivers a much needed comparative outlook and reminds us of lessons learnt along the way. A must read for anyone who wants the nitty-gritty and the fun if social innovation."

- Catherine Fieschi, Director, Counterpoint, United Kingdom

"This is an important piece of reading for anyone interested in driving system level change and learning from the experts in the growing global lab movement. Uniquely written by fellow travellers holding direct experience designing and developing labs, you will take away a set of clearly written stories which illustrate how system change theory can be brought to life."

- Charmian Love, CEO of Volans, United Kingdom

"Social Innovation Labs are spreading around the world, often seen as high-potential vehicles for systems change. But running such labs is not easy. As the authors of this book show, it is a craft. Being lab practitioners, they provide honest insights into their practice, useful for everyone wanting to create a better world."

- Joeri van den Steenhoven, Director, MaRS Solutions Lab, Canada

"Social Labs are an important frontier in global efforts to make progress on complex social, political, economic, and environmental challenges. As such they are the subject of much trial, error, confusion, and learning. This book makes a valuable contribution to this exciting new field."

- Adam Kahane, Chairman of Reos North America and author of "Solving Tough Problems: An Open Way of Talking, Listening, and Creating New Realities"

"Changemakers of the world unite...and buy this book! Labcraft brings engaging stories and thoughtful insights from the front lines of social change. Drawing on experiences of pioneering labs in Europe, North America, Asia and Latin America, this book empowers social innovators to fix their aspirations on systems changing solutions to tough societal challenges."

- Tim Draimin, Executive Director, Social Innovation Generation (SiG) Canada

"A timely, accessible yet sophisticated contribution written by practitioners for practitioners. Packed with stories and accounts of first-hand experience, this short volume brings to life the work of labs and will be a great resource for all those interested in this new exciting way of promoting social innovation."

- Davide Nicolini, Professor of Organization Studies, Warwick Business School, formerly Senior Social Scientist at the Tavistock Institute, United Kingdom

"An inspiring dive into Labs' world. A fresh, coherent and illuminating effort to share the essence of these surprising experimental places for social innovation."

- Sebastian Gatica, Director, CoLab UC, Chile

This is a very topical book. Under significant reform pressure, our institutions have responded by trying to extend existing logics. But more and more they are waking to the realization that a better tomorrow will emerge by developing new logics. Labs are a critical discourse in enabling this transformation to flourish.

- Marco Steinberg, Founder, Snowcone & Haystack, Finland

Labcraft

How social labs cultivate change
through innovation and collaboration

A Natural Innovation Publication

Edited by

Hendrik Tiesinga and Remko Berkhout

Co-Authored by

Mariko Takeuchi
Rachel Sinha
Marlieke Kieboom
Kimon Moerbeek
Lena Hansen
Magali Marlin
Anna Lochard
Josh Harvey
Eduardo Jezierski

Labcraft Publishing
London & San Francisco

Labcraft is published under Creative Commons
Attribution-Non Commercial 4.0 International License.
You may share and adapt the material from the book with
appropriate attribution. You may not use the material for
commercial purposes. You can read the full license at:
www.creativecommons.org/licenses/by-nc/4.0/

First Edition July 2014
Version 1.2 September 2014

Labcraft Publishing is an imprint of
Natural Synthesis Ltd
London, United Kingdom

ISBN 978-0-9905927-2-3 (ebook)
ISBN 978-0-9905927-0-9 (paperback)

Produced by Natural Innovation
Creative strategy by Simone Poutnik
Copy-editing by Lucy Flood and Robyn Landis
Book design and illustrations by James Redenbaugh

TABLE OF CONTENTS

Part 3. Lab Strategies

FOREWORD
BY DAVID EDWARDS, HARVARD UNIVERSITY

Labs are surprising places. Just think about it. We invest money, time, and unusual human effort in projects whose outcomes we see as fundamentally uncertain—in the hope we will learn something we could not have guessed.

We could invest those same resources in work that's more obviously productive—say, building homes, or bioremediation. Yet we choose to invest in labs.

It's not that learning matters more than doing. But we've concluded that doing without learning is, somehow, a bad bet.

When Apple Corporation spends 3 percent of its net sales on lab research, it's betting on the value of experimentation and learning—just as, comparably, the U.S. and Japanese governments bet on that value by spending respectively 2.7 percent and 3.6 percent of GDP on research and development.

Apple cannot predict the future, nor can the U.S. or Japan. And so they invest in efforts to discover it.

The traditional research lab performs scientific experiments within relatively well-defined conditions. Their work is aimed at outcomes that intrigue corporations, governments and nonprofit organizations so much that the latter agree to pay for the experiments. These entities fund experiments in the hope they will learn how to do what they do in ways better aligned with the conditions and needs of tomorrow.

Sometimes laboratory activity is conducted inside the organization itself. Frequently, as with most academic research, funding moves laterally from the organization hoping to benefit from the research to the lab proposing to do it. Systems—including those set up by venture capitalists and entrepreneurs—are put in place to help "translate" useful learning from labs in the direction of funders' interests and society generally.

Thanks to such experiments and research over the past few decades, human conditions have radically changed in many obvious ways. Not all of these ways have been positive. Some have bred confusion.

As a response, a new kind of lab has emerged. And that is the story of this special book. The labs described in these pages approach complex social and cultural problems, often framed by poorly defined conditions and rarely underpinned by traditional scientific method. They bring unusual groups of specialists and interests together to confront questions that transcend the interests of a single corporation or country. And they often conduct their experiments in direct dialogue with the public.

Their approach, indeed their very emergence, parallels the rise (and one hopes, success) of the Internet. Just as the Internet provides a forum for dizzying idea exchange and experimentation, these cultural and social labs are becoming public forums with a potential to spark radical grassroots cultural and social change.

While grass-rooted and as yet unproven, the phenomenon of the social innovation lab is already a matter of large-scale interest. Too many educational, political, cultural and industrial institutions remain fixed to a worldview that is behind us. Thankfully, many leaders are now questioning how their institutions—of all sizes and types—can move to a more contemporary high ground.

The productive function of society has long been based on the effective distribution of knowledge, services, and products. We have come to know what to teach, what to produce, and how to serve—at least in part because we studied and experienced how things worked sufficiently to learn how they might work better, or at least well enough.

Today, we are simply less sure. It's reasonable in these times to question the value of teaching calculus, or making a certain computer, or providing a particular kind of health care—tomorrow.

The cultural and social lab addresses issues, causes, and interests that are not addressable in standard translational labs or inside traditional institutions. Their form, model, and ability to produce positive social change are all in motion.

These are early days for social labs. But, as captured in these stories— written in intriguingly time-constrained conditions, these new labs are asking questions whose answers matter to us all.

David Edwards
Harvard University
Founder, Le Laboratoire
Author, The Lab: Creativity and Culture (Harvard Press 2010)

PART I

INTRODUCING LABS

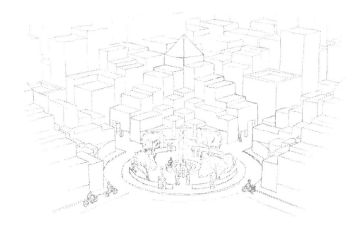

RISING FROM THE RUBBLE

W e live in an era of great challenges and unprecedented opportunities, institutional failure and inertia, breakthrough innovations and technological change. It's an age of painful endings and hopeful beginnings. It's a time that feels as if something profound is shifting and dying, while something else wants to be born.

The playwright, poet, revolutionary, and former Czech president Václav Havel captured the transitional nature of our time in these words:

> *"I think there are good reasons for suggesting that the modern age has ended. Today, many things indicate that we are going through a transitional period, when it seems that something is on the way out and something else is painfully being born. It is as if something*

were crumbling, decaying, and exhausting itself—while something else, still indistinct, were rising from the rubble."

Many of us live in a highly institutionalized world that, on the one hand, meets many of our everyday needs and provides us with much of our wealth—yet which on the other hand deprives and restricts others and creates a host of unintended negative side effects.

Our carbon-based energy systems, for example, create mobility and heats our houses, yet also creates climate instability and geopolitical risks.

Our education systems fulfill upon the fundamental right to education for many, and strive to embody the pursuit of human potential. However, they also produce workers for a 20th-century industrial economy, workers who often burn out or otherwise fail to find satisfaction, meaning, and purpose in their work.

Our health-care systems extend lives, but they're not financially sustainable, nor do they necessarily improve quality of life.

These institutional behemoths seem like skyscrapers—powerful, enduring, and rigid structures that dominate the landscape. And yet these skyscrapers must somehow evolve and change to create space for the new and better systems that want to be born.

However, the skyscrapers are just one side of the story. In the alleys and on the sidewalks, in homes and schools and parks and the multitude of spaces between and outside of institutions—and even in the elevators and hallways of skyscrapers themselves—seeds of transformation are germinating.

The diverse collections of people who are sprouting these seeds find themselves with comparatively few resources with which to develop alternatives. They may work from outside existing institutions or within them, but either way they're often in need of spaces in which to experiment with alternative approaches. Many of these radicals either choose to or are unable to work within the confines of conventional structures. They may be marginalized or ignored.

Our labs are one solution to the challenges such pioneers face. They work to bridge the gap between these disconnected worlds by translating ideas and resources from one world to the other. This book was conceived to illustrate the ways in which Labcraft—the work of such labs—can do just that.

Our labs are part of an emerging family of hybrid organizations that call themselves social innovation labs, civic labs, or system innovation labs and many other adjectives. Incubators, i-teams, hubs, and accelerators are also part of this wider family. In light of this diverse nomenclature, as well as the diversity of labs covered in this book, here we simply refer to them as labs, or "our labs," as these are ones with which we are most intimately familiar.

This is a unique kind of laboratory—one that creates a dialogue, listening carefully with an open mind to all the voices, and then tries to translate them, mix them, and amplify them to prototype and develop alternatives. We cross-pollinate new methods, approaches and perspectives between groups. We provide oxygen, fresh ideas, and protected space to enable new things to emerge.

Our labs coexist with many paradoxes. We have to answer to power—we sometimes *represent* power—and at the same time, we seek to challenge it. We embrace exploration and inclusivity, yet we're ruthless in maintaining our focus on what works. We engage with both the radical and the established, while remaining credible to each.

Tension and ambiguity are inherent aspects of working in this fragile context. There's a craft, an art and a science to creating and evolving these spaces *in between* in order that the *new* might emerge.

It's a craft we hope to uncover, illuminate and question in this book.

THE STORY OF THIS BOOK

Over the last decade, labs for systemic, social, and environmental innovation have risen to prominence—in impressive numbers and on a global scale. Through steep learning curves, they've produced notable and inspiring results. At the same time, labs have lagged behind in documenting and sharing their emerging insights and evidence of their impact.

Efforts to catch up on that front have recently produced a number of insightful papers, books, and meetings about labs. However, we found that too little attention in these was being paid to the *practices* of labs. How do labs view their craft? What do they really *do*? What do they struggle with?

This gap has partly to do with the lab practitioners themselves. Immersed in the work of their labs, few find the time for reflection and sharing, let alone documentation of lessons learned. Moreover, while a lot of learning seems to be taking place *within* labs, historically there hasn't necessarily been much interaction *between* them.

In search of new strategies to promote knowledge production and learning by labs—and between labs—Natural Innovation teamed up with Hivos and the Warwick Business School with the aim to fill this gap through a Book Sprint, a rapid and collaborative book writing methodology. This project brought together 12 different innovation lab leaders, designers, and facilitators to co-create and collaboratively write this book in four days.

This Book Sprint was facilitated by Adam Hyde, founder of the Book Sprint methodology and an accomplished open-knowledge platform designer.

Originally we envisioned that each lab would write its own story, followed by a joint conclusion. But the Booksprint process produced something quite unexpected.

As we started writing, reflecting, sharing, and talking about our experiences, an integrated communal conversation emerged to form the main structure of the book. This conversation developed around several key themes, angles and issues that also formed the backbone of this structure.

As a result, you'll find more than one "we" represented in this book, as each part of it was written, re-written or co-written by multiple authors. Sometimes "we" refers to collaborators from within a single lab; sometimes it refers to a combination of collaborators across several labs.

And though we found many similarities between our approaches, this book does not promote a one-size-fits-all approach to labs. The intention is to describe and share our collaborative work, rather than offer a consensus on "how things are" in the field of labs.

The labs you'll get to know through this book are Kennisland's Education Pioneers, La 27e Région, inCompass Human-Centered Innovation Lab, InSTEDD's iLab Southeast Asia & Latin America, Rocky Mountain Institute's Electricity Innovation Lab (eLab), The Finance Innovation Lab, and UNICEF's Innovations Lab Kosovo

There are already many books that describe methods for human-centered design or multi-stakeholder innovation processes. Our goal is not to duplicate these works. Nor is it to provide a tidy guidebook. Instead, we seek to share stories, anecdotes, and insights from our day-to-day work as labs that—combined with existing literature and your own experience—will allow you to further your own theory and craft of labs.

While writing this book, we had long discussions about who we wanted to write this book for. In part, it's for ourselves, to learn from each other and compare our experiences. We also hope that this book will give our partners and stakeholders a better understanding of our work, methods, and challenges. But most importantly, we want to stimulate the emergence of a community of practitioners who inspire and learn from each other.

It wasn't easy to find a middle way between speaking the brutal truth and indulging in promotional hype. We came to the conclusion that *asking the questions that feel right, trying to be as honest as possible, and telling stories* would be the most useful approach.

That's why this isn't a smoothly polished book, with rounded, structured arguments promoting a singular approach. For example, you'll find sections disagreeing with one another.

But in the spirit of co-creation and iteration that characterizes our labs, we decided to share our learning as quickly and openly as possible. A rapidly changing world requires rapid knowledge-sharing and production, not final answers.

We trust that our findings add to the debate and the development of better practices. We're confident that your feedback will lead to better insights. And as this community grows, we intend to co-create new opportunities for practice sharing.

MEET OUR LABS

B efore we dive in, we want to introduce ourselves, the labs and conveners of this Book Sprint. Throughout the book, we'll be sharing our experiences and stories to help bring the world of labs to life.

At **The Finance Innovation Lab,** we seek to accelerate positive change in the financial system. Launched in 2008, in the wake of the largest financial crisis since the Great Depression, The Lab was co-convened by World Wildlife Fund-UK and ICAEW (The Institute of Chartered Accountants in England and Wales).

We seek to create conditions that enable a new financial system, one that serves people and the planet, allowing life to thrive. We do this by connecting and scaling entrepreneurs who are creating alternative financial business models, civil society leaders advocating for financial reform, and intrapreneurs (people who seek to create change inside mainstream organizations and institutions) in mainstream finance who are repurposing their professions. We run four major programs, reaching over 3,000 people.

At **InSTEDD's iLab Southeast Asia and Latin America iLabs,** we bring together parties who otherwise might never find common interests—large, powerful, mainstream organizations and systems and smaller, more nimble, and unconventional ones. We design technology to improve health, safety, and sustainable development. And we build on the combined strengths of mobile operators, governments, technology companies, opensource groups, NGOs, village health workers, and—ultimately—the people who benefit from the work.

Our iLabs offer a framework for experimenting with sustainable innovation. That framework includes solutions that achieve social impact in new ways—discovered and developed with, by, and for local people—using self-sustaining business models running under autonomous leadership.

At **Education Pioneers** we started off as a fresh rebellious idea to empower teachers, designed in 2008 at the office of social-innovation think-tank **Kennisland** in Amsterdam.

The idea—a support system to help teachers innovate their own educational environments—was a direct response to the conclusion that decades of innovation in the Dutch educational field had failed. They failed because they were all large, top-down projects, and their failure resulted in general fatigue and even anger among teachers regarding innovation.

Although teachers hold a pivotal position, they felt they lacked the mandate to really address the needs of their students. Constrained by national policy, they felt disabled to negotiate those needs "on the ground," on a daily basis.

We try to reposition teachers as central agents in innovation and development of education. We do this by providing them with knowledge, tips and tricks, a learning network, and a platform for their ideas, along with financial and physical space to experiment.

Although this approach directly challenges the organizational and institutional logic of the field, established parties in education are showing increased interest. At this point, we're increasingly supported by many different "old system" voices that understand that new ways of development are inescapable.

Rocky Mountain Institute convened the **Electricity Innovation Lab (eLab)** in 2012 to enable and accelerate transformative change in the U.S. electricity system towards clean energy. RMI recognized that the electricity system's physical infrastructure, and the regulations and business models that govern its operation, are becoming increasingly outdated. They're not addressing or keeping pace with society's changing needs, customers' shifting relationships with their utilities, and technological innovation.

To create a new path forward, eLab brings together incumbents and insurgents within the U.S. electricity system—voices often in conflict, including customers, solar companies, NGOs, electric utilities, and regulators—to enable true system transformation and solutions to challenges that no single actor can address alone.

To do that, eLab is building a platform for innovation. This involves convening dialogues and innovation workshops, building the capacity of change agents in the system, and running a set of projects that design, test, and implement innovative new regulatory, business, and institutional solutions.

La 27e Région was born in 2008 in response to what we considered to be the dead end of the ideology of "new public management," which attempted to rationalize every decision public managers made and operated the public sector like a factory. Although the public sector did undergo some deep transformations in the 1990s and 2000s, when there was some reform of this management ideology, in France public administrations are still like skyscrapers—remarkably hard to change.

We aim to create a shift in administrative culture to improve the quality of public policies. We see public administrations as places potentially full of life and opportunities. We quietly and in a friendly manner "break into" these structures, bringing with us civil society's energy, along with its designers, hackers, artists and social entrepreneurs.

We ensure that public servants who want help creating change can find a place with us. Our ambition is to bring about reconciliation between citizens and their political institutions. We support the design of fair, humane, and sensible policies for citizens.

The **Innovations Lab Kosovo** is a relatively autonomous unit of **UNICEF's** (the United Nations Children's Fund) Kosovo[1] Program. As such, we operate within the enormous apparatus of UNICEF and the wider constellation of United Nations agencies.

Together these organizations comprise the definitive "skyscraper" in some ways. They pair unparalleled resources, expertise, capacity, reach, and political might with often burdensome, labyrinthine bureaucratic apparatus.

Innovations Lab Kosovo and its sister labs across the world are an attempt by UNICEF to introduce new and emerging methods, technologies, practices, and principles that advance efforts to safeguard the rights—and save the lives—of children and young people. We seek to achieve this both within the organization and with our partners.

At the same time—and maybe most importantly— the Lab represents a recognition by UNICEF that it does n't have all the answers. Instead, for young people with new ideas who themselves take on the role of driving social change, the Lab offers access to the resources, capabilities, and reach of UNICEF.

inCompass Human-Centered Innovation Lab is a semi-autonomous innovation lab that lives within **iDE**, a international NGO. Our mission is to deliver breakthrough solutions for the poor by pioneering and advocating the best practices in human-centered innovation.

Our lab uses best practices in innovation to design

---

products and services that improve the lives of the poo in developing countries. But even more crucial to our mission is our advocacy role; our impact is limited if we try to solve one problem at a time. We recognize an urgent need to shift the mindsets of the movers and shakers in the social innovation sphere—those in the "skyscrapers."

We know first-hand that human-centric design (HCD) approaches—those that treat the poor as real customers with a voice—lead to breakthrough and sustainable innovations. Our goal is to build and convey success stories emerging from this approach, and to advocate for these best practices.

Our lab brings together the brains, methodology, and diverse tools for human-centered innovation. We connect these to the financial resources of the "skyscrapers"—companies, philanthropic funders, non-profit organizations—to give the poor a voice in designing solutions that resonate with their needs.

Natural Innovation was founded in 2009, with a vision to foster the conditions for new answers to emerge to the formidable challenges and opportunities of our time. We began buildinlvg on our experience as co-founders and facilitators of labs in a range of fields, from finance and food to social enterprise and organizational change.

As a social enterprise, we now specialize in incubating and facilitating multi-stakeholder innovation labs and networks. We partner with governments, businesses, multilateral institutions and civil-society organizations to develop strategies that cultivate thriving innovation eco-systems.

Inspired by nature, we're convinced that real innovation arises in the creative tension that exists between different elements of a social ecology. We cultivate the right conditions for diverse groups of people to come together to co-create meaningful alternatives.

Over time, Natural Innovation has evolved into a network of collaborators based in Europe, Africa, and North and South America, where we support the development of local multi-stakeholder innovation labs and networks.

Our passion for learning and research inspired us to bring together colleagues from around the world so we could co-create this book—and deepen our understanding of the diverse practices of social labs. Our role in this book was to do what we do best—bringing together amazing people around big ideas, fostering the right conditions for creativity, and delivering concrete results.

Hivos is an international NGO with a 40-year track record of supporting social movements and civil society organizations. We promote open and sustainable societies in over 30 countries around the globe.

For several years, we have backed the emergence of labs focused on technology for development, transparency, accountability, and cultural entrepreneurship. We believe in the potential of labs to address systemic challenges, but we also see labs as one manifestation of open societies reinventing themselves by reshaping the public sphere.

Our involvement in this book stems from our Civic Explorations Knowledge program, in which we study labs as a new phenomenon of civic action. Our interest in Book Sprints is part of a search for new methods of knowledge production, in which activists and practitioners of development interventions take center stage.

As you can see, our labs work in a wide range of fields and arenas, and in different countries and contexts. We have distinct approaches and represent a diversity of worldviews and objectives.

At the same time, we recognize one another as peers, working in similar ways. We share the same passion for changing outdated systems; the same aspirations and doubts about what we are doing; the same vision for new ways to make those changes. Collectively we have many years of experience, and we want to share with you what we've learned.

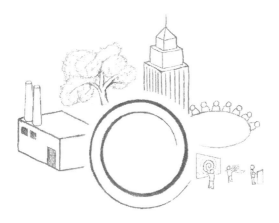

OUR LAB APPROACH

O ur labs arise from the recognition that existing institutions are often poorly equipped to respond to the massive challenges and opportunities we face in the 21st century—those that are complex, messy, fast-moving and non-linear.

Often we see that institutions were built based on a certain set of assumptions that no longer hold, that conventional approaches cannot keep up with the rate of accumulating change, and that well-meaning change agents are spinning their wheels. We also see that for many of the complex challenges we face, no off-the-shelf solutions exist. For example, we have never been faced with a problem on the scale of climate change, or a world-spanning highly interconnected and fragile financial system.

Our response to this uncertain future is to generate new innovations, or to accelerate emerging innovations, that respond to these complex challenges and equally to high-potential opportunities. This is what makes a lab approach fundamentally different from other interventions that are based on pre-determined solutions and plans. The innovations we work with cover a broad spectrum, ranging from public policy, business models, and best practices to new products, consumer behaviour, values, and cultural norms.

A lab approach is not warranted in every situation; there is no value in designing and innovating new approaches where effective responses and solutions already exist. However, in a fast-changing world, even tried-and-tested approaches that were once effective are rapidly becoming outdated.

And, as seasoned activists have learned, creating large-scale shifts demands extreme perseverance and a long-term approach. That's why we see the need for stable and open spaces for innovation that take the long view.

One way of understanding a lab is to see it as a hub or a platform that seeks to catalyze emergent innovations in a particular domain—through diverse strategies and interventions.

This book is divided into three main parts. In this first part, Introducing Labs, we discuss what makes a lab approach different from other approaches to social change, zooming in on two crucial aspects; emergence and inquiry.

In the second part, Lab Space, we explore this platform aspect and look at some of the adaptive and dynamic conditions and infrastructure needed for labs to thrive. We ask the question "How do we organize for emergence and innovation?" The third part, Lab Strategies, discusses the variety of ways in which we're trying to catalyze emergent innovations. We focus on strategies such as seeing the bigger picture, cultivating connections between diverse stakeholders, staying close to people, taking an experimental and iterative approach, enabling and connecting change agents, tracking fuzzy impacts, and staying nimble.

Before we dive into those more detailed aspects, we want to clarify one of the core features of a lab-based approach—inquiry and emergence—and how, through our lab work, this approach ripples out into new domains.

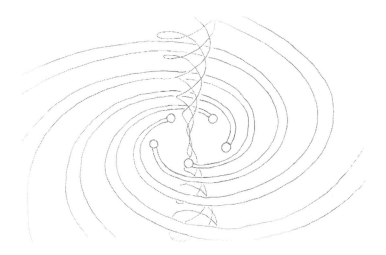

INQUIRY AND EMERGENCE

Supporting the emergence of innovations is at the core of any lab approach. We can't predict beforehand what our programs will create. That's the nature of innovation. Our work doesn't start with a predetermined plan or answer, but with radically questioning the parameters of the existing way of doing things.

We do this by, for example, asking big questions about the values that underpin an existing system, connecting with the needs and interests of the end-users when we design, or bringing in experimental methods that shift the way people within the system see it.

Innovating thus requires that we refrain from trying to converge too quickly on an answer. Rather, we need to allow time for consecutive phases of exploring and evaluating, diverging and converging.

Further, the entire process of framing, exploring, and finding solutions is guided by—or co-created with—the people who are affected by or involved in the problem at hand. We don't define the strategy for solving the problem up front, but rather we do so while synthesizing the needs, motivations, and mindsets of our users and stakeholders.

After really honing in on the questions that matter, we aim to prototype and iterate possible innovations and interventions. Our mantra here is "fail fast, fail often, and fail early." The reality is that complex problems often require a wide range of ideas and approaches and these will need to be tried, tested, and overhauled or adjusted many times.

Being able to react to stakeholder feedback is crucial to designing solutions that will be "sticky" and adopted. That means that flexibility must be built into this step to enable breakthrough innovation. It also means that predicting exact outputs and an exact roadmap for this iterative journey is impossible, given that the intention is to remain malleable in the face of unpredictable findings.

When we launched The Finance Innovation Lab, during the 2008 financial crisis, the co-conveners ICAEW and World Wildlife Fund-UK suddenly found that we had a great deal in common. We started with the question "How can we create a financial system that sustains people and the planet?"

Our first approach was to bring different people in the system together. We wanted to convene a micro-cosm of the "whole system" and then work on an intensive process with senior leaders to identify specific acupressure points that could "tip" the system.

But after a series of events, we realized that we were not going to be able to raise the millions of pounds necessary to sustain such a process. We had also failed to gather the senior leaders around the table who we'd initially hoped to bring together.

So we shifted focus to work with what we had, rather than what we didn't have. We tried a much more emergent, bottom-up approach. Our mantra was "go where the energy is." In our case, that meant growing a community of people in our network who felt a sense of personal purpose to change the system.

That was the turning point, after which our community evolved rapidly. Three groups emerged: pioneers, advocates, and intrapreneurs.

Pioneers were the people building exciting alternatives outside of the current system, such as complementary currencies, peer-to-peer lending platforms and sharing-economy models. Advocates were people from civil society pushing for financial reform. And intrapreneurs were those who worked within mainstream financial services, who led the slow but crucial changes within the existing system.

Over time, our core team honed its skills in convening people within and between these groups. We started to crowdsource ideas and pilot projects. We learned how to craft acceleration and incubation programs to strengthen the capacity of the most promising leaders in our community.

As our network and track record grows, we find our lab increasingly in a position to influence policy and spread its practices to similar initiatives in other sectors. Today our network contains hundreds of organizations and thousands of individuals. As a byproduct, we find that we have to negotiate increasingly complex power dynamics. But we have a clear strategy and strong sense of what works and what doesn't in our context.

At InSTEDD, our work arose out of an idea to connect the world of information and communication technology with tough real-world problems. For us, the Internet is not merely a tool. It's a way of thinking in terms of distributed networks and open architecture.

How do we apply this thinking in humanitarian crises, for example? When big disasters hit, 90 percent of the response is local. Survivors rescue fellow citizens, deal with immediate relief, and then find strength to pick their lives back up—with or without outside support. Information is key for effective frontline responses. Where to look for shelter? What diseases to be mindful of? Where is additional support needed?

At InSTEDD, we saw potential to build an information system to make this potential a reality. We worked with Thomson Router Foundation to build a technology that would enable mobile messaging after a crisis. We wanted to create a system that we could deploy rapidly even in the most difficult of conditions.

This required us to convene and negotiate with a wide range of actors across the globe: mobile operators, the United Nations, and the humanitarian community. It was an intense process, consisting of convening, prototyping, and a set of tests around the world.

When the earthquake in Haiti struck, we were ready. Our teams from iLab Latin America teamed up with local phone companies and UN clusters to deploy within 24 hours. The open architecture of the system allowed rapid connection to crowdsourcing translation and coding. We connected with citizen stringers in affected areas, and tailored messages for the survivors to stay healthy, work with each other on reconstruction, and collaborate with the health system.

An evaluation showed that a remarkable 75 percent of the thousands of recipients did something differently than they would have otherwise, thanks to the messages they received. If 75 percent of the population can make even one small change, the overall impact is unimaginable.

LABCRAFT

THE RIPPLE EFFECT

All of our labs work to amplify change in the current system by spreading our mindset and our approach to innovation. We do this in a number of ways: influencing key leaders in the system, engaging stakeholders in the innovation process, and teaching new approaches and mindsets as case studies.

In recent years, thousands of people have participated in our programs, heard and read about our work, watched our videos, and supported us. In this way, we're functioning as a catalyst in disseminating a new way of approaching challenges, of thinking and doing.

Around us, we see many spin-off labs—lab-type projects inside and outside organizations—and innovators who are shifting the "how" of approaching societal challenges. We could call this a movement, a swarm, a network, or an ecosystem of innovators moving broadly in the same direction.

We're adopting a similar approach, and brick by brick transforming the mindsets that dominate the skyscraper landscape of which we are a part.

This is the larger systemic change we're pursuing. Beyond solving complex challenges, empowering change agents, and creating new solutions, we're seeding new ways of seeing the world and creating alternatives. And we're creating ecosystems that support those new perspectives.

In 2008, when we started La 27e Région, we were a new player in the public innovation world. At that time we felt quite lonely and eccentric, even though we met other pioneers on the way. Seven years later, hundreds of civil servants have radically changed the way they see their missions and their jobs after participating in our programs. We've worked with half of the 26 French régions, three of which have now set up their own labs as a result of our program "La Transfo."

Counties and cities are also joining us. At the national scale, we've helped Marylise Lebranchu, the Minister of Decentralisation and Public Sector, to set up a national public lab called "Futurs Publics." Practitioners are getting on board, and we've built a community of around 50 professionals who are passionate about the transformation of the public sector.

Our contributions and outcomes will continue to emerge, but already we have an original, desirable and recognized philosophy and approach for modernizing the public sector.

At inCompass Human-Centered Innovation Lab, our experience was similar to that of La 27e Région. Within the first year of our lab's existence, we realized that when organizations worked with us on projects, they became absolute converts and advocates for the human-centered approach to designing for the poor.

It appeared that up-close experience with human-centered design naturally and powerfully "sold" the concept. We realized that any future strategies for spreading our approach to movers and shakers in the sector should incorporate this "seeing is believing" insight.

This led our team to ask the question, "How can we give more people the same 'seeing is believing' experience—without having to spend a full year working on a project with them?"

With this in mind, we designed an intensive two-day Human-Centered Design case study workshop. This workshop allows participants to act as human-centered designers on a real-life case study. Participants experience the HCD mindset and tools—and the tangible breakthrough ideas and solutions that arise from applying the HCD methodology.

We have since tested and iterated this HCD Workshop with audiences that range from large NGOs to grassroots social enterprises to seed-stage social entrepreneurs to development consulting organizations—educating an incredibly broad audience in human-centered design.

PART II

LAB SPACE

What's needed to connect skyscrapers and sidewalks in new and innovative ways? In this chapter, we reflect on the anatomy of our labs. We'll provide insights into the ways in which we build, organize and fund our work.

What do the characteristics we described in the previous chapter look like in practice? Our labs intend to offer in-between spaces to enable new connections, ideas, and initiatives. Yet how we deliver on that intention is largely dependent on how we structure ourselves and build our networks, and how we deal with hard-nosed issues related to governance, physical structures, and funding.

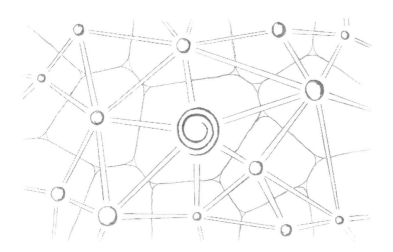

NETWORKED STRUCTURES

L abs aren't actual "laboratories" in the traditional sense of the word. But the spirit is the same. We create a physical or virtual space where people can come together to learn, experiment, and tinker—in this case with new structures, regulations, or products that solve the big challenges we face.

Most of our labs are to some degree dispersed and movable, and they arise around people rather than places. We see ourselves more as "meshworks," or network organizations, that come together in different ways at different times depending on context and the challenge at hand.

Our networks stretch across three tiers:

- A core team leading the lab
- A network working with, for, or around the lab (mix of institutions and people), and
- The wider field or ecosystem(s) within which the lab works.

One of the differences between labs and more traditional forms of organizing is that in labs, the boundaries between these tiers are permeable. Most of our labs have a salaried small core team and some kind of board structure. Beyond that, we find diverse ways to build networks, ranging from paid membership (such as in the eLab) to communities organized through online platforms (as in the case of InSTEDD).

Sometimes a network develops accidentally, but most of us engage a very deliberate process of cultivation. What might start as an informal set of meetings to understand a problem turns into an assessment of who needs to be involved to address it, and then a lot of "pounding the pavement" to get those people engaged.

Building extensive networks is also a key tool that allows us to be flexible and adaptable, convening the best people for a particular task quickly when needed. Physical centers of gravity help, but we believe a strong network needs more than one hub.

The InSTEDD iLab Southeast Asia has evolved through many phases. We've invested in our ecosystem as deliberately as in our own team. This has allowed us to grow our networks and circles. We ultimately work with, hire people from, and send people to learn something from those networks and circles.

For example, to find local leaders in the technology space, we organized barcamps where participants determine the agenda and share what they know with others. Barcamps provide great opportunities for current and up-and-coming influencers to meet and exchange ideas.

To inspire talent among young local leaders and to assist them in sharing their experiences, we helped foster ShareVision, a volunteer-led, knowledge-sharing network between graduates and students.

To identify creative people working in hardware and original start-ups, we invested in Hackerspaces located around innovation hotbeds such as Phnom Penh, so that changemakers would have a physical space in which to run into each other.

To surface local entrepreneurs and regional investors, we sponsor Startup Weekends, Social Innovation Camps (SICamps) and other entrepreneurship events, where we contribute to pitches that have social impact. We hire recognized leaders from other private companies to act as coaches and mentors.

Our core team then connects and brokers initiatives and coalitions across this fertile eco-system to deliver on our innovation mission.

About 20,000 miles west of Southeast Asia, similar dynamics are at work at The Finance Innovation Lab. We distinguish between four interconnected communities that we consider part of our lab.

Our community of interest includes individuals who are loosely interested in the activities of the lab, and come from across the financial system. They might come to one of our Assemblies, sign up for our newsletter, follow us on Twitter, or watch one of our films or Prezis.

This community is useful for us strategically because they amplify our work. Because they're aligned with our intention, they can help us spread news about positive change within the financial system, and help change the climate of ideas.

But it's important that we turn ideas into demonstrable solutions, and so a second community is our "community of practice." We have a series of accelerator programs designed to bolster the leadership skills and strategies of people who are committed to changing the financial system, to demonstrate that an alternative is possible.

Here our community splits into three groups: pioneers creating alternative business models in finance, advocates from civil society seeking policy reform, and intrapreneurs from mainstream financial services. These groups are small because the work we do with them is intensive and much more expensive than hosting a one-off event.

We very intentionally build these communities so that participants leave more like deeply bonded friends than peers. They meet informally and help each other out long after our programs end.

Another group is our "community of influence." These are people who have already created alternative business models in finance, or who are in civil society and are working towards change. We help them come together to form strategic alliances to advocate for specific policy changes that would benefit them all, or to meet with senior policymakers at a workshop hosted by us.

This community is highly strategic and comes together for mutual benefit, but can disband quickly after a reform has been accomplished if necessary.

Finally, our core team builds the strategy of the Lab and nurtures each of these communities. We have spent a great deal of time deepening our relationships, because one of our key learnings is that a strong core becomes a positive attractor for others. The more we understand each other, know our strengths and weaknesses, the better work we do and the more the lab flourishes.

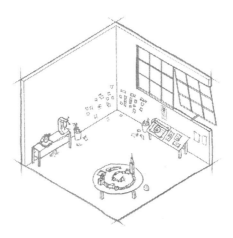

SPACE TO CREATE

Regardless of where a lab is physically housed, we all agree that the look, feel, and functionality of the space is fundamental and can be a distinguishing characteristic of labs. We seek collaborative, flexible, open spaces that help rather than hinder the multiple types of work a lab may do.

If someone gets an urge to jump up and draw a picture, they must be able to. If we modify a process on the fly and move from a big group to breakouts, chairs must be instantly rearranged and tables moved out of the way.

The global image of labs might be one of expensive modern spaces full of high-tech luxury design and Macbook Pros. That's not necessarily the reality. At inCompass Human-Centered Innovation Lab our initial lab space was an old Cambodian home that was poorly converted into an office with a one-window room and terrible lighting. The daily swarm of mosquitoes that started at 4 p.m. left the team uninspired and wanting to work at nearby coffee shops.

We considered becoming an office-less organization as a short-term option, but decided that we needed a physical space close to our partners and clients where we could work together as a team.

We knew that we would be putting makeup on a pig, but we worked imaginatively to make the most of what we had. We painted our room in bright colors, we brought in plants for inspiration, we set up homemade movable white-boards around the room, and we created an open-concept space with one large homemade white-board table for the team to sit around.

As our network and track record grew, we were able to move into a somewhat larger office at a nearby creative co-working collective. This has made a world of difference for our team's productivity and energy in the office. We surround ourselves with photos of our work. We have flexible workspaces that allow for project work and creative sessions. Our infrastructure is slowly improving.

Yet in the Cambodian context we have to be mindful of perceived elitism. We have made a conscious decision to live with this tension and build relationships in other ways—for example, by inviting partners and clients for lunch. It's also important—both for our work, and for these relationships—that we spend much of our time in the field.

Defining a lab's space starts with the actual places we occupy on a day-to-day basis. And here we have some different perspectives on what's preferable. Some of our labs are housed within a "parent" or partner organization's facilities. Being co-located with a parent can signify important support, and if the lab interacts with that organization frequently or shares staff, it makes movement and meetings more efficient.

On the other hand, for some of us, being co-located risks compromising neutrality. For example, if a particular foreign funding agency pays for the space, or if a government ministry hosts the office, our work may be linked to theirs by association. Association with a larger institution can bring with it both positive and negative connotations.

The Finance Innovation Lab is a joint venture between ICAEW and WWF-UK, and our core team is physically located across two different offices. This has become challenging as the project grows in size. There are times when it would be great to just lean across the table and ask a quick question, and it's hard to build team spirit when people are in different locations.

But on the upside, this challenge has called us to become particularly adept with Skype, Google Hangout, and Dropbox, working on our own and then coming together for a day and getting lots of strategy work done at once. It's actually quite efficient.

Being located at ICAEW's offices has been massively beneficial to the project, too. The building is right in the heart of the city where most of our stakeholders are based. It has lots of conference rooms we can use, from an intimate Victorian library to boardrooms, and a huge conference suite that fits over a hundred people. Generally we've been able to use these facilities for free. Because our strategy has always been about convening the system, we would've really struggled without it, especially in the early days.

Another challenge of being physically separated is that we can sometimes risk appearing elitist or exclusive. Given that labs are tasked with "doing things differently" than the parent organization, operating in a location physically separated from the main body of the organization can reinforce a feeling of distance and "otherness." This is exactly counter to the inclusive and participatory nature of labs, and can threaten to undermine a lab's very purpose.

At the Innovations Lab in Kosovo, we've been on something of a "space odyssey." We started in a modular, open-plan space outside of the host UNICEF office. The space reflected and supported the culture and practices of the lab: openness, accessibility, agility and responsiveness.

The space was immensely appealing to the young people who were our target stakeholders, but over time we discovered that our bean bags, colorful couches, and general vibe were actually alienating to our government partners, who constituted another significant part of our change equation.

Moreover, the stark contrast between the UNICEF main office and our Innovations Lab Space complicated our objective to foster innovation "on the inside." We needed to recalibrate.

Through partnership with the Municipality of Pristina, we were able to split our lab into a small office next to our headquarters and an open space in the heart of a nearby burgeoning neighbourhood. While this was a small change, we found it immensely instructive. We learned that space matters, that it's political, and that it can move us closer to or further from partners depending on its constitution and location.

These examples show that most labs implicitly or explicitly work with the principle coined by architect Christopher Alexander that "form follows function."

At the InSTEDD iLabs, for example, spaces are always adjusted to suit the evolving trajectory of the labs' development. Back in 2008, the iLab Southeast Asia had bedrooms that allowed for core teams to work together intensively in low-cost fashion, to save on expenses when engineers and experts came together for capacity building, program design and staff scouting for months at a time.

But as our network started to become more important, we moved to an open-plan working space in a building that hosted a lot of hi-tech companies around what locals called "the silicon stairwell." This allowed us to hold joint demos and create opportunities for knowledge sharing. We share the iLab space with volunteer organizations, technology groups and others who need it in the evenings or on weekends.

A lab's location often help to define its brand, differentiate its approach, and make it clear to participants and visitors alike that we're getting ready to do something different. The space a lab occupies or creates can make an important statement, and our craft is represented in part by how we repurpose and design space to enable our work.

Most of our labs conduct the bulk of their activities in a multitude of venues outside of the office. These can include fieldwork sites, retreat settings, and a variety of convening spaces. Here, we need the personality and culture of the lab to extend to these events.

At Education Pioneers, we pay a lot of attention to the spaces where we hold our events. We want to emphasize and recognize the innovation and leadership capacity of teachers. So our teachers get to share the final presentations about their innovation processes at the castle of a prominent business university in the Netherlands. This university is generally perceived as the epicenter of entrepreneurial leadership. For the teachers to take the stage in such a special space is a conscious and symbolic gesture that expresses the importance of teachers as leaders in the education system and society at large.

Learning lab sessions, however, take place in schools—to emphasize that this is where the innovation really has to take place. At these sessions, education pioneers come together to learn from each other, evaluate their projects, and define new strategies for the coming period. We support them with inspiration and guidance.

At first these sessions took place in Kennis-land's office—a chic building in the historic center of Amsterdam, which is perceived as the geographical area for the Netherlands' cultural and intellectual elite. As the program kept growing, we consciously chose to move the learning labs to a particular school that is among the frontrunners of education innovation in the Netherlands.

While eLab is primarily managed from Rocky Mountain Institute's offices in Colorado, its most important spaces are the external venues that host its collaborative meetings and workshops. Finding the right venue turns out to be an art form—each of eLab's three to four meetings per year are hosted in different parts of the country to highlight regional activity.

One of eLab's main goals in terms of space is to put people in different physical settings so they can see things in a new light, and to support them in really "showing up" to meetings.

To help create that space, venues are usually located in nature, away from a city center, and the dress code is casual. This practice has bordered on scandalous for some established business participants, who have a hard time leaving their suits and ties behind.

The main meeting room is usually twice as large as normally required for the group's size, to ensure attendees have flexibility to interact in different ways. It also usually has plenty of daylight and a low-key vibe.

Overall, eLab values space that is flexible and functional—space that easily supports and adapts to the needs of the meeting, rather than forcing participants to adapt to the space or feel limited by the confines of a conference table.

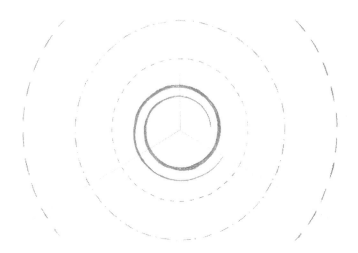

PERMEABLE BOUNDARIES

The previous chapters begin to reveal how in our labs, the boundaries between "who's in" and "who's out" are permeable and ever-changing. People and organizations may come and go from our teams and networks, depending on the specific problem we're trying to solve and the stakeholders to whom it's relevant.

The flexibility to call on different parts of a lab's network and ecosystem is critical. To make the most out of our network potential, we're learning to use multiple lenses, and to be ready to quickly integrate those different viewpoints.

At the Kosovo Innovation Lab, we're constantly mixing and re-imagining our units and team. For instance, some of our best insights for new campaigns haven't come from advocacy experts, but from our software engineers. We build mechanisms expressly to diminish these boundaries—including the "fences" between UNICEF and partner staff, and between the Lab and the young people we work with and for. We're rowing a big enough boat that anyone who wants to hop in need only ask for an oar.

At Education Pioneers, we follow this strategy right into the "boardroom" of our lab. Our main partners—unions, the education ministry, and regulatory bodies—are all part of our project team. Engaging those partners in the project team is a conscious strategy. It distributes the ownership of the program and embeds its results in the system we wish to transform.

Peers working in more institutionalized settings often ask how we deal with the downsides of permeable boundaries. They point at the confusion created by constantly changing shapes, structures, and dynamics, and ask how this impacts the communities and people who interact with the lab.

And indeed, we ask ourselves many questions related to this issue. Because a person attended a lab event, are they a member of that lab? If a consultant works closely with the core team, do they become part of the core team? If a community is no longer strategically aligned with the work of the lab, how do you gracefully exit from or disband that group, after the lab has worked to build connections with it? How do we deal with ownership of knowledge and outcomes, and with issues of confidentiality?

Our labs have certainly not found final answers to any of these questions. We're instead learning to deal with confusion and new sets of ambiguities in new and constructive ways.

We've discovered that our labs have employed some common approaches that align with our values of fostering networks and celebrating diversity of contribution. These approaches include creating fellow networks, giving people space on shared blog posts or visibility in social media, and recognizing alumni on websites.

We plan proactively to deal with ambiguity, so that we avoid spending significant time on ad-hoc relationship management or confusing our partners with convoluted roles and relationships. That kind of confusion could send mixed signals and expectations to future network members, who might wonder how they "fit."

At The Finance Innovation Lab, our core team plays an important role as an attractor for new projects and in cultivating strong relationships with stakeholders and collaborators. One of the most painful parts of running our lab has been learning how to draw a boundary around the core team of the lab: when to let consultants in to help us design strategy, and how to shift that relationship when it's no longer supportive. There's also the question of whether and when to replace core team members if they're absent. Questions surrounding inclusion and exclusion are part of an ongoing learning process.

At La 27e Région, our small core team of seven people can only be successful on a relevant scale because we work with a network of around 40 independent professionals that we have carefully developed over the years. We call them "residents" or "partataires" (a mix between the French words for "partners" and "contractors").

We function as a "platform," setting up experimental program in which partataires get involved in small teams working in the field. We build those teams and hire those people mainly through informal processes. While this keeps us agile and flexible, it also makes us quite vulnerable and requires a high level of confidence.

We're currently working on formalizing our relationships through proper contracts and rules. Finding the right balance is challenging. We also try to strengthen and mobilize this community through different channels: annual open meetings, regular group sessions during programs, and regular email and social network communication. In this way, we create a strong network with a friendly atmosphere that's essential for our collaboration.

ADAPTIVE RESOURCING

As labs, our ability to achieve our objectives depends greatly on the resources we can bring to bear on those efforts. Here, we use the term "resources" in the broadest sense—the staff, skills, competencies, funding, and partner support that collectively empower our labs to act.

Labs are building alternative approaches to conventional ways of doing things, and this context demands that every part of our infrastructure be agile and adaptive.

We work on adaptive resourcing in two ways. Firstly, we cultivate networks of partners—peers, collaborators, and donors—that understand the nature of our craft. At their best, they serve as an external support apparatus that is adaptable and can respond to needs and take advantage of opportunities as they emerge.

For example, Innovations Lab Kosovo sits within a network of invested partners. The lab can draw on that network to fill gaps in competencies and capacities as shifting objectives demand it.

At eLab, we recently faced an acute challenge: we needed lots of additional facilitators for an unusually large workshop that we had been able to broker among regulators, utilities, technology companies, customers, and environmental advocates. Because eLab is housed within RMI, we were able to leverage RMI's staff and quickly marshal the resources we needed to do the work. It's these kind of adaptive resources that have made all the difference to the success of our lab.

Through constant improvisation, our labs build core teams whose members possess a breadth of skills and capabilities, and who value and practice flexibility and agility. Labs' approaches, and the context in which labs work, demand a receptivity to transition and a comfort with ambiguity. This means our teams must be able and willing to look and work across disciplines—including those notably different from theirs—to marshal resources in creative ways. Our teams must value the lab as a container for a multitude of capabilities and perspectives.

At Education Pioneers, we have developed two particular types of adaptive capacity. One is a necessary flexibility regarding the process of obtaining funding and/or a mandate to execute a program.

We've lost count of the unforeseen delays and unexpected periods of acceleration that come about when working with education authorities. More than once, it took months before some commission officially decided to assign funding. And it's nothing less than a mystery when we might finally get a definitive "go."

Moreover, it's often expected that when a mandate does finally arrive, your organization will kick immediately into gear. Funding partners frequently seem to expect that everything should have been in place yesterday. We've learned, often the hard way, to deal with planning and finances flexibly.

We've also become a lot more assertive with our partners. We stretch beyond capacity to make our multi-actor initiatives work, but we have also learned to say no or to take a firm stance when progress is willfully being obstructed.

The second adaptive ability that has been essential to our work comes from having a set of interdisciplinary competencies. We've learned to deal with a broad range of tasks and challenges. More than once, it's been greatly advantageous to have just a few people dealing with broad issues such as campaigning, communication, overall project management, graphic design, group processes, and so on. This kind of skill breadth makes it possible for a small organization to have a relatively large impact.

Finding the right people to fit this interdisciplinary profile can, of course, be difficult.

At InSTEDD iLabs, we spend a lot of time scouting and coaching team members. Internal culture and external relationships are fundamental to how we work, so we prefer to have positions empty than risk having the wrong person.

We look for people who fit in the culture of self-improvement, collaboration, and sharing skills and knowledge; people who share our values, and who eagerly jump into the opportunity to develop expertise in diverse areas. If you're looking for a stable office job with a clear role and mandate, you're not going to find it here.

Our engineers are constantly in the field prototyping and improving solutions. We actually refer to the role informally as "muddy boot developers." And to build empathy with workers at the larger institutions, we might partner with or swap team members, or co-locate at their offices—for example, spending two days a week in a Ministry of Health.

And when local support is needed in other countries where we don't have iLabs, we train companies there to build a local network and give them opportunities to do the work. This frees us up and keeps us focused on our core mission.

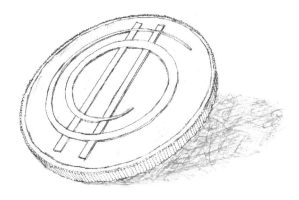

LAB MONEY

L ab work costs money. Materials, travel, salaries, research and development, and rent: all need to be covered to meet our long-term plans to change things systemically.

Each of our labs works with different revenue and funding models, and most of us are constantly exploring new models. We all share one perspective: the revenue and funding model is not merely a footnote about how we obtain resources. It's a fundamental design choice that affects and defines how the labs pursue their mission. The revenue and funding model will set incentives and disincentives, establish credibility or damage it, and create freedom or restrictions.

We balance the needs of participants, voices, and stake-holders in our labs, maintaining a degree of autonomy and freedom, while trying to meet our own needs for financial sustainability. As a result, most of us have hybrid funding and revenue sources. Among us, we have a mix of four distinct approaches. These include:

1) Project funding from the private sector, public sector, or philanthropy in return for specific deliverables from the lab.

2) Relatively unrestricted funding that the lab can decide how to allocate.

3) Membership fees, where stakeholders who derive value from the lab's activity pay one-time or recurring fees for different levels of participation and services.

4) Financial or in-kind support and resources from anchor organizations of which the labs are a part. This can include, but is not limited to, in-kind or subsidized supply of physical space and materials, operations efforts, and advisory support from external groups or "parent" organizations such as institutes and universities.

These forms of revenue each have their advantages and disadvantages, and bring both constraints and freedoms.

Not all labs are set up to accept all forms of revenue—tax structures, overhead of parent organizations, and other factors differ vastly across our labs. In addition, the origin of funding sources such as grants and capital investment can matter to a particular lab: such sources can include private philanthropy, impact investment, commercial venture capital, or corporate social responsibility. Again, each one has pros and cons, which will vary depending on our mission and type of organization and ecosystem.

Not all of our labs aim to raise their own funds. If a parent organization is happy to provide much-needed support, many of us are happy to be able to focus on our work rather than spend time finding ways to fund ourselves.

About 50 percent of core costs for The Finance Innovation Lab are funded by its two parent organizations
WWF-UK and ICAEW. This includes the core team's
wages, office space, free rooms for events, and a lump
of funding each year that goes towards projects.

But external partners fund the majority of projects
within the Lab. The UK Government Cabinet Office, for
example, funds our new business model incubator. The
Big 6 audit firms fund AuditFutures, and foundations
like Friends Provident and Calouste Gulbenkien have
funded our work with our policy reform community.

eLab's mixed funding model leverages three
approaches. First, a set of philanthropic grants fund
the eLab core, platform, and more than half of its
project work. Second, membership fees—on a sliding
scale (ensuring that funding is not a barrier to entry, as
eLab brings together organizations with vastly different
resources)—contribute to the work eLab members want
to do collectively.

And finally, some projects—or aspects of larger
projects—are funded by fee-for-service work. This
shared funding model for projects allows eLab to push
the envelope on what's possible. It enables an independent perspective rather than relying solely on a
single entity's near-term business priorities, while still
ensuring that participants have "skin in the game."

At InSTEDD, it's key to our mission that we support users of our technologies in employing the most appropriate and relevant tools. This requires that we keep a constant watch on trends so we can prepare for them.

Back in 2010, we saw that mobile phone penetration was going to be reaching every household within five years, but that literacy wouldn't catch up fast enough. This implied that voice-based phone calls were going to be critical so that we could maintain personalized, two-way interaction with the populations we try to serve. To do this we would need open-source, highly scalable gateways based on protocols like VoIP (voice over Internet protocol).

But the up-front investment needed to design such tools was not affordable from our operational overhead exclusively. And we tried and failed to portray the value of this potentially transformative new technology to USAID and Rockefeller Foundation.

In the end we had to take a "stone soup approach" and bring together a combination of seed money from Google.org, CISCO, and a passionate community of project implementers who were willing to invest "once it worked"—such as Grameen Foundation—and recover costs through mobile operator licensing agreements.

Today, the tool that emerged from this effort is serving millions of people, and it's thrilling to see NGOs imagining new forms of interventions based on this tool.

Karl Brown from the Rockefeller Foundation reflected back to us why it's difficult for them to deal with the kind of requests we brought to them regarding this technology project:

"We're approached regarding funding for many good or even great ideas, but it can be hard to find funding for them if those ideas aren't closely aligned with a strategy we're already pursuing. Strategies and budgets get established every so many years—the process is quite complex internally, and isn't purely driven by abstract analysis of net benefit. If Rockefeller Foundation's efforts and portfolios had at that time better matched the project, we might have been able to fund a project with such potential.

For the InSTEDD iLabs, regional autonomy is an important principle. Over the years, our approach to building revenue has changed as the organization and its products evolved and matured.

Originally, at iLab Southeast Asia, we were supported with philanthropic funding from Google.org and Rockefeller. After two years, we wanted more flexibility to choose which projects we worked on, so we started diversifying to include more projects from local partners. And because we want iLabs to have a reinforcing feedback loop with their regions to ensure our services are locally relevant and valuable, we strive to support our iLab work with regional revenue only.

Six years in, being funded through projects still creates a big risk for cash flow and lack of stability. Philanthropic projects for social impact don't have predictable funding cycles, and politics is often more important than value in that funding ecosystem. We're now 90 percent project-funded, with all projects from regional sources, and all business development done by iLab itself.

To cover the rest and add stability, we are seeking more product- and subscription-based revenue. For example, we took technologies that we were using for social projects and licensed them to telecom operators for monthly fees or revenue-sharing agreements.

Our labs are relatively young. We all expect to continue to explore revenue models, so we can increase our freedom to stay creative, neutral, and stable. But we all fear stagnation and misalignment. We worry that we may get too "stuck" on the models we choose, and that we may not be able to jump into new ones in the future, or that they may create a set of incentives and disincentives that dilute the mission.

We agree that we wouldn't allow even the most self-sustaining and profit-generating activities to distract us if they weren't fully compatible with the ever-changing nature of the lab. We'd rather spin them off or license them to others.

The diversity of funders and funding modalities is our best bet for preserving autonomy and freedom. Autonomy and freedom in turn are crucial for working on the complex problems and ecosystems we live and work within.

This need for freedom manifests in different ways:

Neutrality. Our labs need to adapt to the context and changing landscape of players and powers. Depending on the problem and context we work in, we need funding choices that can change over time. Some revenue sources bring agendas and may compromise our neutrality or the perception thereof.

Stability. To build core team capacity, relationships with our networks, experience and predictable staffing resources, in addition to developing new products and offerings, our labs need to have some level of stability over moderately long time-frames. Not having enough "horizon" in funding or unstable cash flows and staff, restricts labs that set out to have long-term impact.

Flexibility and creativity. Often the projects that can make the most difference come up unexpectedly, or what we learn necessitates a quick change in focus of a project. This requires some ability to quickly source new funds or get approval to reallocate funds or risk missing important opportunities for impact.

PART III

LAB STRATEGIES

I n this section, we take a closer look at our strategies for generating and accelerating emergent innovations and approaches.

We don't claim ownership over all the approaches that lie at the heart of our craft. Many are pioneered by others, and are employed widely and to great effect by a host of practitioners in a variety of fields and contexts.

Our interest in this section is what happens when our approaches are at work in practice. We've picked eight strategies that we will further unpack.

We start with the importance of "Seeing the Bigger Picture"—understanding the larger context and inter-relationships in which we seek to intervene.

We then explore "Cultivating Connections," weaving relationships between diverse stakeholders to create new insights and understanding, and creating fertile ground for collaborative innovation.

"Staying Close to People" focuses on the importance of localized, context-specific learning about what is really needed by end-users or affected populations.

From there we move on to "Experimenting and Iterating" and "Empowering Change Agents," where our approach becomes more tangible in experiments and projects. The chapter "Tracking Fuzzy Impacts" focuses on the challenges inherent in having to answer to traditional performance measures while working with innovation.

"Labwashing" explores the dilemmas we face as we engage with power and politics.

We close with "Staying Nimble," the foundation for staying agile and open for emergence.

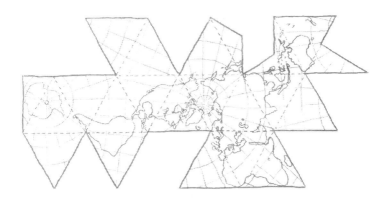

SEEING THE BIGGER PICTURE

M any of our labs start with stepping back and trying to understand the landscape in which we are
operating, and the interconnections between
various players, rules, and stakeholders.

Social systems are vast and complex, and individual organizations can sometimes forget that. As intermediaries and
conveners of diverse stakeholders, our labs have an opportunity to make a larger part of the system visible to all, or to help
that system see itself better.

Imagine, for example, the Eiffel Tower. A photographer
stands before the monument and snaps a single photograph. From that photograph, we can learn a good deal about
the Tower's architecture and structure, its location in the city,
and its interactions with tourists.

Now imagine every person in Paris, no matter where in
the city they are, turns a camera to the Tower and snaps a

photo. Imagine how much more we might understand about the Tower from that enormous set of photos than from a single perspective.

In a similar sense, overlaying a diversity of seemingly disconnected perspectives lends an otherwise impossible depth and dimension to our collective understanding of a problem or situation.

Seeing the whole system helps people and institutions that are normally immersed in it to see the forest rather than the trees. When people are able to broaden their view, even just a bit for a short period of time, and look at the system as an observer, an "aha" moment is much more likely to arise. And for any of us, it can be empowering to realize that we aren't the only tree trying to change the forest.

Finally, mapping the system can help us identify the emerging alternatives, and any barriers to their entry. It can also be useful to map the ecosystem of change initiatives that are trying to tackle the problem on which we're focused. Understanding system dynamics can help us see the leverage points where we might best intervene.

At The Finance Innovation Lab, for example, we convened a group of entrepreneurs from the emerging peer-to-peer lending market in the UK. The number one shared characteristic in this group was *exhaustion*. They worked alone, building innovative business models, and inventing new legal structures as they went. They applied to the government for a license to operate and were refused or delayed for months on end. They had no bandwidth to lobby for change.

We convened the community to identify where the Lab could intervene to support them. They stood together, sleeves rolled up, frowning to read the wall of Post-it notes in front of them. We'd mapped the emerging alternatives to mainstream finance bubbling up in the UK system: complementary currencies, crowdfunding, and peer-to-peer models, among others. We'd created a simple diagram, outlining the regulatory changes that would allow these markets to flourish.

The community helped us pick the one thing that would make the biggest difference to them—regulation.

We sensed that the timing was right. The market was growing significantly and we knew that politicians and policymakers were warming up to the idea. We created a joint charter signed by the growing number of entrepreneurs in this space and submitted it to government. At a Lab event a few months later, a spokesperson from the Treasury stood up and launched new regulation designed to support our pioneers.

"It's all about the chicken!" This was definitely not a statement we expected to hear in the first meeting of a group of senior executives from the electricity industry—especially not accompanied by animated gesturing towards a Lego chicken on a table. But this seemingly random declaration became a turning point in the meeting.

We were holding our first eLab meeting. We had convened electric utility executives, regulators, solar entrepreneurs, large commercial customers, and environmental advocates in an attempt to understand the current situation in the U.S. electricity system—and develop strategies for how we could most effectively intervene.

These very busy businesspeople normally spent almost all their day-to-day time talking, typing, reading, and otherwise using their minds. We wanted to see what would happen if we invited them to explore, in a different mode, the challenges they saw in the industry.

So we put them at a table with a big pile of Lego in the middle and asked them to first individually build a model depicting a key challenge they had personally experienced, and share that with the other people at the table. Then, to iterate this exercise, they were asked to build a *collective* model for how the group saw the challenges of the current system.

Out of this exercise came a new take on the role of the regulator in enabling change (symbolized in the model by the Lego chicken)—an insight that shaped the conversation for the rest of the meeting.

eLab constantly reminds participants of the importance of getting physical—using their hands to build physical models out of Legos; actively collaborating at white boards and flip charts; taking paired walks to build relationships and trust, share ideas, and have meaningful conversations. In contrast to many other industry meetings where people's energy often gets deflated, finding multiple ways to work with that energy changes the flavor and quality of the conversation—and new ideas, insights, and opportunities emerge.

Seeing the bigger picture isn't always straightforward or helpful. It can also be paralyzing to map out a system as far as we can.

At the beginning of each Education Pioneers year, we always draw a visualized map of the education system that surrounds a teacher's idea—starting in and around the school and branching out from there.

One teacher spoke out when looking at the map of his system, saying, "I don't feel like doing anything any more. My director seems to be afraid I will spend all my time on developing my innovation. The government inspectors might not like what I'm doing. And the parents might not see the relevance."

So one danger in seeing the bigger picture, as in this case, is that we can become overwhelmed by the sheer size and scope and complexity of it all. It can make us feel that any action we might take is irrelevant. When people see the whole system, they run the risk of becoming discouraged from trying to innovate.

To forestall this dynamic, it's crucial for a lab to guide people towards positive action. Our EP team connects teachers four times throughout the year on "lab days," organized either at the schools or at Kennisland. Online they're connected in a Facebook group. Further, the EP team also gives and receives feedback through coaching telephone calls, and visits the schools twice throughout the year. The teachers value both online and offline meetings as vital support.

Many large systems don't have a clearly defined scope, and it's often difficult to draw the line regarding where to focus. What has the greatest impact—linking up innovations across regions, or focusing on a very specific geographical area?

In the U.S. electricity sector where eLab does its work, one of the characteristics that most influences our work is the structure of the sector itself. The U.S. appears to be one country with one electricity system. But in reality, the contiguous U.S. electric grid is actually three major but fully separate grids.

What's more, electricity is regulated by states, so it's almost like having 50 electricity systems, with some 3,000 utility companies spread across those 50 states.

How does a lab influence a system like that? This was a question we wrestled with, and argued about, as we designed eLab.

We could have focused on the national level to engage the best thinkers and most progressive decisionmakers from around the country, but that would risk a level of abstraction that would keep us away from the on-the-ground reality and our opportunity to drive real action.

We also considered focusing on one or more specific states, but that would risk creating strategies so specific to an individual state that they could not be scaled. One approach was too broad, the other too narrow.

In the end, we've taken the middle road, working across multiple levels. Our core eLab group comes from around the country, but our eLab Accelerator teams work together around regionally-specific projects.

And our eLab projects span the range—we produce high-level discussion papers designed to shape the thinking of the entire industry, and we work on on-the-ground projects. Like what's happening in Fort Collins, Colorado where we brought together experts from the region and around the country to support the city in creating a downtown zero-energy district through conservation, efficiency, renewable sources, and smart technologies.

By doing both, we're trying to create a learning cycle where industry-level thinking informs what can be tested in specific places. And then we use what we learn from those places to continue to evolve the larger conversation.

In some ways, too, this is part of our evolving theory about how to stay nimble—by not being tied to a specific region, we can quickly flex our focus to the areas that need it most. We can also assemble a diverse set of projects that produce better insight.

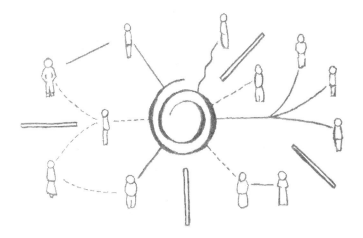

CULTIVATING CONNECTIONS

T he practice of cultivating connections is an enormous part of our labs' work, which begs the question: connections between *whom* and *what*?

Our labs often bring together people who don't—or can't, or won't—normally engage with one another. We facilitate interactions between actors from differing sectors and fields, divergent backgrounds, and distinct, frequently antagonistic factions in our societies.

Often, we do this to uncover commonalities. These engagements commonly end with a remarkable alignment of needs, challenges, and aspirations. And—equally valuable—a shared understanding of points of divergence and conflict often emerges.

It's essential to build understanding of opposing perspectives, and build depth and strength of relationships. Each of these outputs constitutes an important brick in the foundation of our prospective interventions.

Bankers and anti-capitalist campaigners working together to imagine a future financial system seems impossible—and yet that's the kind of interaction we foster at The Finance Innovation Lab.

Likewise, at eLab, we believe that what's required to drive change is solar companies discovering common ground with traditional electricity giants, and coming together to create joint experiments on new pricing models.

In other cases, our labs drastically dis-intermediate structures of communication and power by bringing end-users together with the institutions responsible for delivering on their basic rights.

New options and solutions open up when InSTEDD's iLabs convene meetings between directors of health ministries and HIV patients. They discuss a new mobile tool that would allow doctors and health workers to alert each other to medication needs.

When inCompass facilitates grassroots human-centered design experiences for corporate executives in Cambodia, it immerses participants in the realities of life at the bottom of the pyramid. This makes new markets visible, and demonstrates that strategic design *must* have input from users at the grassroots level in order to create win-win solutions.

At The Finance Innovation Lab, we brought together over 100 accountants, investment bankers, anti-capitalists and design students and used open-space technology to crowdsource ideas for a better system.

Over a hundred people wearing pinstripe suits and cords, summer dresses, and sneakers stood in a circle on a sweaty summer day. A facilitator asked, "Step forward into the middle of the circle and read out your idea for a better financial system."

An awkward silence followed, until a shortish American guy with brown hair and glasses took a breath and crept forward, bent down and scribbled on a Post-it note. "I'd like to host a conversation on natural capital," he said quietly into the microphone.

This is how we started. We hosted many more events like this one, and they built the critical mass of community, ideas, and momentum that brought our project to life. Now six years old, our project has a network over 3,000 people and organizations.

When we convene a breadth of actors, we bring together not just a diversity of people but also a diversity of perspectives, ideas, and capacities. We know from post-event feedback that to most participants this is the most valuable part of our events—bringing together people who don't normally talk to each other, in a space where they can discuss things they care deeply about.

eLab often functions as a catalyst for new connections that drive innovative solutions. Several years ago, one of its members—Fort Collins Utilities, a municipal utility in Fort Collins, Colorado—decided it wanted to be a national leader in clean energy. Its first step was to establish FortZED, a zero-energy district designed to produce as much energy as it uses.

That vision was a start, but not enough. So Fort Collins' municipal electric utility joined eLab asking what it could do to facilitate a process that would lead to further action.

An eLab innovation workshop brought together Fort Collins community members with national eLab experts who might never otherwise have looked so closely at the city, the community's energy system, and potential leverage points for change.

The city began working with RMI and eLab on two key questions: 1) How far and how fast could Fort Collins reduce its carbon emissions and move towards a clean, prosperous, secure energy future? And 2) what innovative new approaches could the utility use to help its customers more easily adopt energy efficiency and solar energy?

Now, a year later, Fort Collins is building an action plan for how it could achieve 80 percent carbon reduction by 2030, and is preparing a pilot project to test an innovative business model that will help it achieve that goal.

Key to this progress was staying grounded in the needs and priorities of the community rather than trying to superimpose goals from national outsiders.

At La 27e Région we try to create safe spaces where highly institutionalized public institutions' members can meet truly engaged activists, who harshly criticize political power. We hope that those unexpected meetings can contribute to changed mindsets on both sides.

We decided that it might be a good idea to work with a theatre company inspired by the Theatre of the Oppressed. In the Theatre of the Oppressed, the audiences explore, show, analyse and transform the reality in which they are living, in order to promote social and political change.

We thought that this would be a constructive way to help civil servants to engage with new forms of civic participation. It appeared one step too far for our partners on both sides, at least at this stage. Civil servants felt they were too aggressively questioned about their skills and practices, without any simple and actionable ways on hand to improve it. Artists from the theatre company were unsatisfied with the quality of the process, feeling that they were making too many compromises. Sometimes you just can't force it.

Yet we're in these processes for the long haul, and what might appear not to be working today could in fact be sowing seeds for more successful interventions at a later stage.

One of Kennisland's main strategies is to start up programs such as Education Pioneers and embed them in the field. As a result, the central Dutch educational authority adopted Education Pioneers and made it part of their strategic agenda. This official recognition provides us with opportunities as well as new challenges.

The opportunity lies in the fact that our institutional partners become co-owners of Education Pioneers, giving our approach and philosophy a bigger platform and potential further growth and dissemination. The challenge is the baggage that such "skyscraper" partners bring. Our innovation-oriented approach is not part of their DNA. Their bureaucracy stifles and restricts our ability to be agile and innovative.

"I've brought the laminated printouts of my business model," the participant said. "But how can we change it, if it's covered in plastic?" said the facilitator. "We want to merge your model with Susan's." "Well, I don't want to," he said bluntly.

Our strategy at The Finance Innovation Lab was to convene people who had good ideas about how to change the financial system and encourage them to collaborate with each other, to merge their ideas and create new hybrids.

We encountered two problems with this strategy. The first was that we had no criteria for selection. We used the principle of emergence and "going where the energy is." But people who have the most energy aren't always the people with the best ideas. If you want to create genuine impact, you also have to orchestrate and pick the people who have the greatest chance of success.

Second, pioneers who have a clear business model don't necessarily want to collaborate. And nor should they. If they have a good idea, the best thing they can do is to stay focused and do what they're doing, and do it really well.

Over time, these are the some of the most important learnings our labs have found crucial to cultivating connections:

Create safe spaces. In labs, participants can come and hear views they don't normally align themselves with; be honest about the challenges they face; and show up as individuals, not the organizations they represent.

Take a birds-eye view. Find the parts of the system that don't understand each other, and look for people doing similar work in different systems. These stakeholders usually learn the most from each other.

Unexpected connections can be the most obvious ones. Sometimes it seems to make sense that two people should work together. And yet, for many reasons stemming from hierarchies and organizational and disciplinary silos, they just don't. At the same time, some pairings or groupings that seem unlikely can become the most fruitful. Don't take any connection for granted; you might miss some excellent opportunities.

Don't wait to be asked. Often we're not given the mandate to convene, but do it anyway.

Pull experience from everywhere. We build unexpected connections across disciplines by

bringing together ideas like social enterprise, personal development, marketing, design, advocacy, and education.

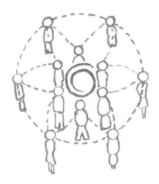

STAYING CLOSE TO PEOPLE

A nother aspect of our lab approach is to work directly with ordinary citizens and users—people. Our goal is that decisions within a system emerge from the authentic experience of end users, and the professionals that represent institutions "on the ground," such as teachers and nurses.

Staying close to people isn't just good practice, it's about respecting the rights and agency of users to influence processes that impact them.

When the InSTEDD iLab started working in Southeast Asia on disease surveillance, we began a dialogue with community health workers to discover what information they could use to more quickly identify and respond to an outbreak.

We started comparing stories from rural health workers with central data, and quickly discovered that traditional disease count reports led to inaccurate information that couldn't be acted upon fast enough.

Using rapid prototyping techniques, we arrived at an alternative set of game-changing behaviors: what if they could chat among themselves in real time, with awareness of their locations? What if they had more opportunities to escalate observations to the right experts, only reporting structured data when necessary?

This led to a suite of mobile tools over Short Message Service (SMS) that we called "GeoChat," which shifted the paradigm for field reporting. Users loved it and the tool started getting used in many countries. Users were able to stay up to date, felt less isolated, and could detect and respond to outbreaks faster than before.

The big test came during Typhoon Ketsana in 2009, when central Thailand was ravaged by a massive storm that caused unexpected floods in poor, isolated areas. The health workers on GeoChat were able to report floods, coordinate rescue operations, and mobilize movement of boats and other resources. Because they had the tool they needed when the unexpected happened, they became the first and only response coordination in their districts.

At inCompass Human-Centered Innovation Lab, we worked with a social enterprise to design a water filter that would provide safe water to rural primary schools in Cambodia. Their starting assumption was that the solution we designed would be funded by donor grants.

But as we spent more and more time in the field working with a wide range of users and stakeholders—primary school teachers, students, and community groups—we saw that more sustainable models might be possible.

We observed that low-income schoolchildren received a surprising amount of disposable income every day—and they were spending it at "school kiosk" vendors to buy colorful sugar syrup mixed with ice or water. Children were accustomed to paying for thirst-quenching products at school!

We also learned that "school kiosk" business owners are key service providers on these school campuses, with an interest in keeping their student-customers happy. They were interested in potentially providing water on a semi-commercial basis.

Finally, we learned that the schoolchildren are the janitors, fixers, maintainers, and cleaners of the school; every aspect of maintenance and clean-up is placed in the hands of physically small children. This meant that any new products—including water filters—we might introduce to the schools would be left to young school children to maintain and clean.

Water filters typically require daily, physically strenuous cleaning and upkeep—making them impossible to functionally sustain at these schools.

How could we use these new findings to create a commercially sustainable funding model, rather than relying on subsidies? And if young children are already overburdened with a range of maintenance and janitorial duties for the school, how could we design a solution that wouldn't rely on them for functional sustainability?

This "emergent" approach to redefining the problem led to a fundamental shift in the project's goals. By identifying existing sources of financing for thirst-quenching products, as well as commercially-minded service providers, we were able to move away from a financially unsustainable donor subsidy model.

And by identifying the unsustainability of any product solution due to maintenance issues, we were able to reframe the project—as a more holistic product-and service design—to ensure that young children would not be burdened with impossible maintenance tasks.

In 2010, La 27e Région started a project in Corbigny, a village in Burgundy. We sent a team to one of those abandoned small train stations to explore the potential behind the remaining infrastructure. The team planned to conduct interviews, create proposals, and test real-life solutions.

But we soon realized that the bigger issue was enabling mobility in rural and isolated areas, in a context where local train stations are shutting down. Decisionmakers are often too disconnected from what's happening on the ground to respond to this reality of limited mobility and its potential impact on the local population.

We decided to involve a local decisionmaker through a small role-play. We assigned him a fictional character and a mission. That's how he ended up as Amanda, a 25-year-old unemployed woman trying to find a way to get to Paris for a job interview. As Amanda, he realized that because of inadequate transportation options, he would miss this job opportunity.

This simple experience was mind-blowing for him. He had an experiential, *felt* sense of what it would be like not to have adequate transportation options. In this way, role-playing was much more impactful for him than reading another abstract report about how many trains are running every day.

This demonstrates how role-plays can serve to help decisionmakers and stakeholders stay grounded and to "put themselves in the user's shoes" in order to understand another's experience. In this case, it allowed a public service provider understand the needs of his constituents and consider how to meet those needs.

Some of our key learnings as we aim to stay close to people are:

Get immersed. The best make-or-break observations often come when the observer is embedded in the target systems and with target beneficiaries. There's no substitute for being there. InSTEDD uses the saying "If you don't go, you don't know." You can also build design skills in people who are already immersed in the context.

Just asking might not get you what you need. Interviews are invaluable, but they're only one tool in the observer's tool kit. Users may lack the schema or even language to communicate their needs. And often they are so intimately familiar with—and invested in—existing narratives about a problematic situation, they may not be best positioned to see what would be clear to a third-party observer.

Build for the hardest to reach. Some labs, particularly those looking at rights and equity issues, encounter the greatest success by solving challenges with and for the hardest-to-reach communities and "scaling backwards" to communities experiencing fewer or less severe deprivations.

For example, working directly with the most marginalized users and staying close to them throughout the design process gives Innovations Lab Kosovo the gut check it needs to continually prioritize robust solutions—solutions that can function even in the most challenging conditions.

Positive deviance is powerful. Staying close to users helps us fight the assumption that we *must make a new thing.* Instead, we commonly find that elements of the overall challenge have already been addressed by community members who successfully developed their own local solutions that deviate from the mainstream way of dealing with the problem. Hence, our efforts are better spent iterating upon and scaling these existing bottom-up solutions than reinventing the wheel.

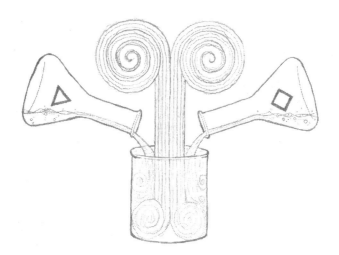

EXPERIMENTING AND PROTOTYPING

The notion of experimentation figures prominently into how we as labs identify and conceive of ourselves. What's a laboratory, after all, without experimentation? We don't just use experimentation in order to develop new solutions; it's in our DNA.

The concept of experimentation in the "hard" sciences is widely understood to involve these steps: look at the evidence; propose a hypothesis that explains that evidence; create a trial that tests the ability of your hypothesis to confirm, predict, or explain the evidence; and use the results of your trial to refine your hypothesis.

This definition satisfies when we're, say, testing for the existence of an undiscovered but predicted subatomic particle, or the interaction of a new drug with human physiology.

But what does it mean to *experiment* in the context of a lab focused on societal questions?

Our approach to experimentation looks considerably more like the natural sciences than a cursory glance might reveal. Using the approaches and methodologies discussed elsewhere in this book, we seek to understand the nature of existing social and environmental challenges. We create hypotheses about how best to intervene in these situations to realize a desired social change, as well as hypotheses concerning the interactions of our solution with and within connected systems.

We translate our hypotheses into prototypes for new or improved solutions to social challenges, often in the form of products, processes, policies, or services. We test those solutions through their application, often in the form of pilots or trials with users. And we use the results of our tests to iterate and to inform the creation of still-better solutions.

And we develop our own strategies and programs through a trial-and-error process of experimenting and prototyping.

At one Finance Innovation Lab event, a friend and supporter came up with the idea of creating an accelerator for social enterprise focused on sustainability. We were in the phase of experimentation, and although it wasn't clear what the connection was between this incubator and our work, we agreed to help. He brought along a partner, a business coach and a strategist who jumped at the chance of supporting the project pro bono, and the four of us set about planning how we could launch it.

We brought our convening skills, and worked with the coach to define what small businesses would need to succeed. We pulled in the founders' contacts in the social enterprise world to attract participants and supporters. The nine-month Accelerator program hosted 10 entrepreneurs and was a terrific success: 80

percent of projects received funding within four months of graduating, and the community was so deeply connected that it continues to meet up more than two years after it ended.

We decided not to run the accelerator again, but we were so impressed with the business coach that we hired her to coach the Lab's core team. With her help, we refined our strategy and created a plan to launch an accelerator that would really create an impact in our sector: supporting entrepreneurs with alternative business models in finance.

We wrote the strategy and shared news of our intention with a few super-connectors in our network. Within weeks, we were approached by the Impact Hub Westminster, who wanted to fund our accelerator as part of a wider bid in The Cabinet Office. The Finance Foundry was thus formed. It was our ability to experiment that allowed us to build our own capacity to host the accelerator.

The prototype emerges as a central feature of our approaches. Whether it's that new, real-time water quality testing device, that multi-stakeholder spatial planning policy, a new pricing model for electricity, or the SMS-based vaccine stock-out reporting tool, a prototype is our hypothesis made real.

It's vital to experimentation that we introduce some *thing* you can test—something real that can succeed or fail, that can go off the rails, that can have unintended outcomes, that can *break*! That test allows us to learn.

There's a ton of great thinking out there on prototyping, so we'll say only this: prototypes are disposable. Create them quickly and cheaply to make your thinking tangible, get it into the hands of users and stakeholders to test it, and throw it out when you've extracted what you need to know in order to make a better version.

Iteration is what we do with that learning: we take our lessons from trials and pilots and feedback loops built around our prototypes, consolidate them into a refined hypothesis, and build a new and improved version of that prototype.

One of La 27e Région's programs—called La Transfo—supports regional councils in building their own locally embedded innovation labs. One of the local councils participating in the program, Champagne-Ardenne, came to us with this question: how can we increase youth participation in cultural activities?

Champagne-Ardenne had already introduced the Lycéo, a card that gives students 20€ to spend on the purchase of theater tickets and other cultural activities. But students rarely used the card, and the officials were at a loss about where to go from here.

The typical answer to this would be to hire an expensive consultant to do the work. But we thought we could use this as an opportunity to experiment with a more sustainable—and possibly cheaper—way to do it.

The actual story unfolded in five days. It began with a user research phase. Trained and guided by our multi-disciplinary team, a group of civil servants armed with cameras were tasked with "tailing" the Lycéo brand wherever it was visible (a flyer at the entrance of a cinema, a poster in a high school, etc.). Photos were collected, captioned, and analyzed to map Lycéo's presence and identify gaps.

On day two, civil servants divided into small groups to reflect upon three key issues: How and where can I get information about Lycéo? What should I do with my 20€? If I have a problem, who can answer my questions?

Day three had teams design four prototypes in response. These were tested in several cultural facilities with students from two high schools. Responses from the field were then collected and analyzed on day four in order to identify and shape tangible proposals for improvement of the card/device.

On the final day, we introduced other members of the organization, discussed lessons drawn from the experience, and submitted the proposals to decisionmakers through a small exhibition.

A few weeks later, three of the five proposals had been implemented, resulting in a radical improvement in the use of the device. But more than anything else, the group had experienced a new and powerful way to work together in an organization that usually operates in a very silo-ed manner.

But experimentation isn't easy, we found. It implies, among other things, finding out the hard way that great ideas don't always work out in practice. As the following example demonstrates, it demands humility—and an ability to kill or genetically modify your darlings.

Massive Open Online Courses (MOOCs) are challenging existing models in education. Innovations Lab Kosovo was asked to explore the use of these models to meet the education needs of marginalized youth in Kosovo, who are poorly served by the formal education sector.

Initial research suggested that while MOOCs go a long way toward providing access to educational material, their impact on educational achievement— whether or not students absorbed, comprehended, made meaning of and used that content—was questionable. Experts in education suggest that people learn best together, yet the structure of these online courses removed this important dynamic. Another factor is that Kosovo's marginalized youth commonly lack access to the Internet.

The lab hypothesised that MOOCs might be more effective if recast as *one* component of a holistic educational experience. We proposed a low-cost, low-tech service prototype: a program that involved light facilitation, using a laptop and a projector that enabled the lab team to take the content of an online course to offline communities.

We brought together young people in youth-friendly spaces in order to reintroduce the group learning dynamic, and built in question-and-answer sessions and panel discussions with local issue experts. We defined a set of criteria for success—simple factors used to assess whether our prototype met the needs of the young people—and we set decision filters to determine when to shut it down.

It didn't work. Student attrition numbers were high. We discovered that this solution failed to account for key elements of the way marginalized youth in Kosovo learn. Our prototype service didn't address the trust dynamic inherent in student-teacher relationships.

For these young people, respect for what is being taught is an outcome of a social contract between the teacher and the learner. It turned out to be extremely challenging to build a relationship between students and the glowing figure on a projector screen. We had set adherence, attrition, and achievement as our key indicators of success, and these measures suggested our prototype had gone off the rails.

We interviewed participants and worked with them to design Mark II. A second iteration included a trusted community member as the facilitator; the introduction of the trust dynamic resulted in us meeting our targets much more successfully.

There are limits to experimentation. For instance, there is an ethical limit to experimentation, as we are experimenting with other human beings.

Teachers who experiment in their schools, for example, usually have little room to fail. Everyone is watching: their directors, their colleagues, their innovator peers, and especially the parents (who in general aren't in favor of experiments in the classroom with their children). If an experiment or two fails, the consequences are usually that either the teacher gives up, or their environment finds a good reason to stop them.

When real problems occur, our project leaders cannot say, "This is not our problem." In a process of trial and error, we as a lab carry a responsibility to offer professional guidance and support. In the case of Education Pioneers, we have to ensure that innovative teachers don't come across as playful or naive.

When experimentation in a school isn't working, we need to help innovators see when to stop experimenting, and change course to a better strategy.

One example involves a teacher who, over several months, kept bumping into limits as she sought to experiment with matching up students with peers in a new way. When she also began suffering from a medical problem, she reached out for help. We supported her in taking a break, during which she was able to make a career switch to another school. We transferred the Education Pioneers budget to the new school, and supported her to start her innovation process again.

Some of the things we've learned over time about experimenting:

Know what you're trying to discover. There's a lot to be said for insights that emerge from pilots, and even more to be said about being open to being surprised. But our experience suggests that our efforts are best served when we define from the outset what we hope to learn from a pilot or trial.

If it isn't working, stop doing it. This may sound obvious, but continuing on with something when it's clearly not working happens more often than you might think in almost every type of organization. One of the key aspects of rapid-cycle prototyping is that you simply stop doing something when you realize it's not working, learn from that, and move on.

Don't take it personally. Labs take risks, so failure *will* happen. As much as we fetishize failure in social innovation, it can still hurt when it happens. Make sure the culture in your organization genuinely supports the notion that things won't always work, and backs up the individuals who lead experiments.

Be strict about learning. Experimentation isn't a substitute for deeper learning. There's no point in failing for the sake of it. It's crucial that no matter how much you may want to forget a failed experiment, you reflect after every activity that went wrong on what went well, what didn't, and what you'd do differently.

ENABLING CHANGE AGENTS

One of the most important principles underpinning our practices is "go where the energy is." We find pioneers and help them get their work done better and faster.

Change agents can come from anywhere. They're the solar advocates trying to make disruptive change from the outside. They're also the intrapreneurial auditors who are working to transform the way their institutions work from the inside. They're the mothers in Kosovo working to have their children immunized. They can be highly skilled or completely fresh. They may have solid institutional backing—or none.

The core philosophy here is that the people ultimately best suited to make change in the system are the people who are actually in that system or those impacted by it—those who live and breathe it every day.

Consider, for example, the average profile of a teacher—a smart, highly educated person with lofty ideals and love for their essential assignment: preparing children to thrive in our society.

But due to top-down policies, teachers are historically simply trained and expected to teach within the existing system, and not to change the educational environment.

At Education Pioneers we empower teachers to reclaim a central position in the development of education and education organizations.

Take Egon, a teacher who wanted to experiment with social gaming in his class. He kept hitting brick walls of colleagues and systems not interested in gamification. He needed to develop a strategy to engage his colleagues and management.

This is where our lab came in. We invited Egon to be part of a community of 20 innovative teachers, and to exchange knowledge online on Facebook, Twitter, and in person during a four-day education lab workshop.

Those four days were completely focused on building four specific skill sets: researching and designing, experimenting and learning, improving the experiments, and making them sustainable.

Before the Education Lab day, we asked Egon and his peers to carry out an assignment: they had to elicit and share stories in their school environment, either making a video or publishing a newsletter or an interview. These stories engaged colleagues in their change projects, and the process of creating them also helped identify new needs. We then used these stories and newly-identified needs to further develop projects in the Education Lab.

After that, we collaborated to address challenges in various ways. We provided personal coaching, peer learning, seed funding, and help in developing a compelling communication strategy. This support helped Egon buy new social games and spread his enthusiasm for social gaming throughout the school and his municipality.

This snapshot of Education Pioneers in action reveals the kinds of methods we use to nurture change. Many of our labs work with processes of incubation and acceleration. As an accelerator, we build a program of support around existing business models and take people through processes to improve and scale their work.

At the Innovations Lab Kosovo, we identified a challenge and opportunity in Kosovo's immense disaffected youth population. We responded by developing the By Youth For Youth program.

A "social venture pre-incubator," BYFY introduces young people—especially youth from marginalized communities—to the principles of entrepreneurship and social innovation. Then it advances their professional readiness through the experience of designing and leading a social impact project.

Design varies considerably from one project to the next, and the lab doesn't presume to tell young people what issues to prioritize. The lab's 120+ youth-led projects tackle everything from using geographic information systems to map gaps in the region's emergency preparedness infrastructure, to creating networks of peer educators among Roma girls and women to increase the community's knowledge regarding sexual and reproductive health.

Regardless of the impact of individual projects, youth leaders almost invariably emerge from the program better able to identify and analyze challenges and take action against them.

This brings us to another strategy: building the capacity, knowledge and skills of a stakeholder group you want to empower. We often use peer-to-peer elements to strengthen ownership and agency.

In Kosovo, young people with intermittent access to water and other basic services are typically on the Internet 24/7. Two young men applied to our lab's pre-incubator program with an observation that the multitude of organisations working with and for youth in Kosovo were completely overlooking the potential of connecting with young people through social media.

That observation led to a project, now called Blue Circle, that provides youth workers with free work-shops on effective use of social channels to reach target constituencies. It became so successful that it evolved into a not-for-profit social media and communications consultancy.

Blue Circle is a great example of the multiplier that's realized when you enable and empower young people to drive change themselves.

Campaign Lab was a leadership program for economic justice campaigners, hosted by The Finance Innova-tion Lab along with two other partners. We recognized that these campaigners are often building huge move-ments while running on passion rather than experience, and that they would benefit from time spent building strategy and leadership skills and learning to take a more systemic perspective.

The program included training from the New Economics Foundation (NEF) about how the financial system works, and workshops designed to build participants' personal leadership skills through self-reflection and mindfulness techniques. It taught systems change theory and practice, and helped participants think about how they could work together to create more impact. We also built a safe community where participants can provide ongoing support for one another.

Some important learnings about supporting change agents:

Create communities of change agents. Participants can learn from each other as well as from you, and they'll have a support system that remains long after you stop facilitating.

Nurture accountability. Where possible, help people who are personally committed to your cause and are truly motivated to learn. People who are "told" they have to participate can be hugely disruptive to the process. Ownership can only be taken, not given.

Be realistic about timeframes. Genuine capacity-building takes a long time. From the start, set expectations regarding impact.

Acceleration is quicker that incubation. If you incubate concepts, rather than strategies or businesses, expect that many ideas or projects won't get off the ground. Accelerators that support scalability for pioneers who are already innovating produce much faster results.

Be clear about what you hope to achieve through capacity building, and let your objectives inform your efforts. In the case of Innovations Lab Kosovo's By Youth For Youth program, in which young people from marginalized communities are supported in taking entrepreneurial action on community challenges, preparing young people to drive the process is far more important than the success or failure of a business or project. In this scenario, capacity building is integral to the Lab's model of sustainable social change.

In other cases, capacity building for the sake of growth can backfire, as we discuss in the section on "staying nimble."

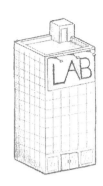

POWER AND LABWASHING

H ow do we navigate the power dynamics between institutions and labs? Central to our craft is the ability to play the game while changing it. In this chapter we explore some of the challenges our labs are facing, and ways to work around them.

The political economy of our labs can complicate matters. In almost every case, part of our funding comes from those very skyscrapers that we seek to change. Sometimes, we're housed within them; in some cases, we're part of them—an embodiment of an institution's commitment to renovating and reimagining itself. Innovations Lab Kosovo, for example, attempts to spread social innovation practices within UNICEF so it can continually reinvent itself. Education Pioneers and La 27e Région work with teachers and civil servants on change "from the inside."

As a result, we constantly walk a tightrope between challenging the status quo and asking radical questions using unconventional methodologies—while not alienating our own supporters and critical stakeholders. Swaying too far one way might make us irrelevant, while moving too far the other opens us to critique of "labwashing" important issues.

An exercise that superficially *looks* like a lab process, but really only touches the surface and avoids really challenging the status quo, actually diverts scarce resources from where they could make a greater difference.

To be successful, we need to "take our own medicine" and critically reflect on how we walk this tightrope.

In The Finance Innovation Lab we've had to be very careful to avoid labwashing. The reputation of the finance industry has been so badly damaged by the financial crisis that many powerful organizations are keen to partner with projects like ours that could help repair that damage in the eyes of the public and business community. We've had our fingers burned on this a couple of times and have learned from our mistakes.

We get around this danger zone by setting strong criteria for partnership; we don't work with individual companies (unless they have a clear mission-driven intent), only professions as a whole. We support innovation in finance, but only that which brings positive change for people and the planet. And we work in partnership with organizations who are committed to long-term change processes, or movement building, rather than one-off events.

At eLab, members recently learned that the cost of rooftop solar and battery energy storage are dropping so quickly that in as little as a decade, it could become cheaper for customers to disconnect from the grid than continuing to purchase electricity from their utility. This would directly challenge the financial health of electric utility companies, many of whom we're working with in eLab.

The challenge is to help these utilities see this potential outcome not as a threat but rather as an opportunity. The essence of elab holds that traditionally incompatible parties—established utilities, and entrepreneurs working on radical alternatives at the margins—are really part of one community. And eLab must remain credible to both. For the eLab core team, this requires diplomacy and flexibility while maintaining a firm commitment to the group's mission.

There's a growing youth participation ecosystem in Kosovo, but its execution tends to be increasingly uneven. For example, one youth participation network, the Local Youth Action Council, is run by and for youth advocates and has become ingrained in Kosovo legislative and municipal structures.

The network is quite successful from the standpoint of engaging youth. But in practice, the system actually fails to represent the *diversity* of Kosovo's youth. It would be easy for the Lab to tolerate this and deliver our services through such an institutionally recognized, sustainable structure. But to slap an "innovation" sticker over a traditional intervention would be labwashing, and it would compromise our mission and mandate as well.

Young people from the Serbian, Bosnian, Roma, Ashkali, Egyptian, and Gorani communities are largely excluded from the programs of the Local Youth Action Council, to the extent that young people within these communities are forming their own alternative grass-roots action groups. The lab is working with those alternative groups to deliver a holistic series of advocacy trainings. These experiential trainings culminate in the development and leadership of a real advocacy campaign, with the support of the lab.

At inCompass Human-Centered Innovation Lab, one aspect of our work is to provide fee-for-service design consulting to those tackling complex challenges facing the poor. Our clients for this service are a mishmash of institutions from the world of "skyscrapers"—philanthropic funders, international development agencies, multinational corporations, nonprofit organizations, and social enterprises.

The only requirement is that our clients have a shared vision to improve the livelihoods of the poor by giving them a voice in the design process. As a social innovation lab, our goal is to spread our way of thinking to effect systems change.

This creates a tension that isn't always simple to navigate—especially when cash is running dry and the existence of our lab may be at risk. Two years ago, inCompass was approached by a new social venture that needed help to design a service model that could significantly improve the agricultural productivity of poor farmers in Cambodia. After many months of working together to finalize the project details, the potential client raised a concern about the confidentiality of information, asking that the project outcomes and key learnings not be shared with the broader world—not even two years after launch.

This left us in a serious dilemma: to lose the project would mean losing a significant chunk of upcoming revenue that we had planned on. In addition, we would have team members with no work to do, which isn't only wasteful but also unmotivating.

Yet taking on the project without any ability to share the learnings would mean that we were taking on the project largely for the sake of the cash. There would of course be the direct human impact that we could have from delivering the project, but the most important part of our work—spreading knowledge—would be foregone.

The decision wasn't black or white; both avenues could lead to compromising our mission. In the end, our decision was influenced by a practical calculation of our remaining cash flows. We had several months of leeway—not much, but perhaps enough to try to find a way to survive the hump. We considered the likelihood of finding additional mission-aligned work in this short period before remaining funds would run out.

Ultimately, we decided that the inability to share our learning would be too much of a compromise to our mission. However, we do wonder how much more complex and difficult the decision would have been had there been even less (or no) leeway in cash. Do we compromise the need to share our knowledge for one project so that we can keep the lab alive, or is this a slippery slope? Should we avoid making even a small compromise, and shut down the lab, knowing full well that this would kill our social impact forever?

This is a fine balance that we believe all labs juggle, and we must rely on a solid moral compass to make difficult decisions that have no black-and-white answers.

Becoming co-opted by power players and structures in the existing system is one of the greatest risks we face. When do we become so immersed in the game that changing the rules becomes a secondary goal? What we've seen across our labs is that these tensions, paradoxes, and questions arise constantly and must always be addressed seriously.

TRACKING FUZZY IMPACT

L et's return to our opening metaphor: skyscrapers, sidewalks, and the in-between spaces that our labs occupy. We've seen the emergence of practices based on connections, ideas, and human energy—practices that sow seeds of change in unlikely corners. In this section, we look at measurement of our practices. We ask "how can we possibly know whether we're on the right track?"

The goal of many of our labs is to change larger societal systems. This doesn't happen overnight, regardless of your approach to social change. We can compare the way we operate to the process of building a magnificent temple: it's a community effort, a channel for creative energy, and people who do it may not see the full outcome of their work in their own lifetimes.

So leading a lab is to some extent an act of faith. We can never be 100 percent sure that what we're doing is actually changing things. And even when we do see undeniable and concrete changes, we can never know for sure if we're changing things in the right direction. But we get the sense that the system is shifting around us as a result of our activity.

More importantly, the sheer fact that we exist in the world is in itself one of our greatest impacts. All labs are real-life examples of how institutions and civil society can work together in more human, democratic, and creative ways.

But the reality is that many of the people we depend upon for our survival—those who help resource us—are waiting for us to explain in clear and measurable terms the difference we're making. For some aspects of our labs' work, this demand is straightforward; in other areas it's significantly more challenging.

Moreover, conventional ways of evaluating impact often require that outcomes are predetermined before an intervention has even begun. Performance is measured against these predetermined targets. This is inherently problematic when you work with emergent innovation. We can often guarantee outcomes—but not which ones.

And predetermining outcomes isn't just practically difficult for a lab—it's also in direct opposition to our very intent and approach. It's inherent to the mission and culture of most innovation labs that we stay open, not draw quick conclusions, and adapt—not begin with assumptions and narrow the possibilities. We value curiosity and fluidity, not rigidity. In other words, even if we *could* approach the evaluation of impact conventionally, we don't really *want* to.

So there's an inherent contradiction between the predictive modus operandi of the existing institutions we work in or with, and the emergent approach that our labs use to innovate. Decisionmakers are generally neither used to, nor comfortable with, hearing us say, "We understand that you feel the problem is such and such, but we want to take two steps back and invest money and time to explore the context with our users and stakeholders."

As labs, we see that a more general exploration of the problem will allow us to understand the nuances and opportunities within the problem space, and help us to define it differently. When we do that, we're more likely to arrive at a breakthrough.

We create different levels of impact. Some are tangible, some intangible; some are direct and some indirect. The emergence of these changes can span decades.

In one way or another, all our labs create impact. And in the best cases, that impact *is* directly measurable.

For example, SMS software developed by InSTEDD allowed families in Haiti to communicate following a natural disaster, and allowed people to access food and resources. Likewise, The Finance Innovation Lab can easily measure and track the number of economic justice campaigners that have graduated from its campaign lab, and subsequent actions they take or projects they produce.

Many of our impacts are less tangible, and yet no less real. One way to understand these less tangible impacts of labs is to distinguish between four levels of impact:

1. impact at the level of the lab itself,
2. the spin-off labs that we generate,
3. the innovations and innovators we cultivate and support, and
4. an emerging new narrative.

1. The Lab Itself

Creating and running a lab is in itself an outcome that we shouldn't ignore. Successfully introducing a new social change approach into a conventional context is no small feat, and represents a significant and high-impact accomplishment.

Imagine, for example, the scale of change required to shift the financial system. At face value, it seems an impossible task. But by its very existence, The Finance Innovation Lab brings a process for reimagining the future. It creates new coalitions and relationships that wouldn't come about in old structures. Auditors talking with conservationists? Bankers talking with design students?

Our labs help create new stories, connections, and experiments, burrowing through layers of change at the level of institutions, societal values, and individual people.

The value of this work lies in expanding the climate of ideas. It creates connections and breathes diversity into systems caught in the trap of "no alternatives." Capturing the impact of these activities in a clear narrative one of our challenges.

A poignant question might be "what *wouldn't* have happened if the lab didn't exist?" This can help to illuminate the role that a lab plays in shifting systems.

2. Spinoffs

Many of our labs have created new labs that focus on other themes or challenges, using a similar methodology.

In 2013, Kennisland was asked by one of the funders of Education Pioneers to develop a new lab program for school leaders based on the principles of Education Pioneers. Inspired by Education Pioneers' work with teachers, we at Kennisland wanted to take this approach to the next level of school leadership. We're now in the middle of developing this new yet to be named "primary school leadership lab."

Likewise, AuditFutures is a project launched by The Finance Innovation Lab to repurpose the audit profession. It began because colleagues at ICAEW, one of the founding partners of the lab, saw the groundswell of innovation being created in The Finance Innovation Lab and were curious about whether the same ideas could be applied to challenges facing the audit profession in the aftermath of the financial crisis.

With the help of The Finance Innovation Lab, ICAEW launched AuditFutures using a similar approach. The project has been embraced by the leading audit firms and has matured into a fully-funded multi-year innovation program that continues to grow.

Each of our labs have inspired or launched spinoff labs, and spread our social innovation practices into new contexts.

3. Innovations and Innovators

A third level of impact comes in the form of developing new solutions, policies, technologies, business models and products (the innovations), and through building the capacity of change agents (the innovators).

The involvement of change agents in our programs can range from intensive retreats and long-term incubation projects to participation in a one-day event or evening drinks. This aspect of tracking participants is a real struggle, as resources are scarce and capturing the impact of the many participants who pass through all of our programs is impossible.

An example of the kind of impact we can create through supporting changemakers comes from Education Pioneers. The innovations that teachers develop might seem relatively small to outsiders, but in the education environment such innovations are significant and can cascade quickly and broadly.

Through qualitative research and evaluation, we were able track how innovations evolved throughout the year. One example involves Sarah and Aysun, two teachers at a primary school in a relatively deprived neighbourhood in Rotterdam. They observed that their pupils, mostly with immigrant backgrounds, had significant problems with the Dutch language—most specifically with reading. Even though this language barrier was generally recognized as a common problem in this part of the city, and reading programs would help, the local library had closed its doors due to budget cuts.

Sarah and Aysun wanted to act. They had the idea of creating a new, interactive, neighborhood-focused library concept within the school. However, the educational field in general usually doesn't provide support for any project that's not part of official policies, normal workflow, or standard school infrastructure.

When they were selected to participate in Education Pioneers, Sarah and Aysun prototyped their concept and put EP's slogan "Dare to Share!" into practice. They quickly sought engagement through social media, printing flyers and spreading newsletters. They understood that it was pivotal to get their colleagues, the parents and the school director engaged. Engagement was also led by the children, who became super enthusiastic.

Sarah and Aysun shared with us that the EP lab days offered them new ideas and a space to share both doubts and enthusiasm. The library and its related activities ended up becoming a highly visible part of the school and the neighborhood. The children became measurably more enthusiastic about reading, and the number of book loans increased. As their success spread, this approach interested other schools and municipalities.

Most importantly, the teachers proved that with just a little extra help and some space to experiment, they were able to act very quickly on an urgent social challenge.

4. New Narratives

A fourth level of impact created by labs is the cultivation of new meta-narratives—the stories through which we understand society and detect opportunities for change. We act as hubs in networks of changemakers and emerging innovations, and from that unique position we can see the new stories emerging in between seemingly diverse projects and ideas.

For example, a core piece of The Finance Innovation Lab's strategy is to illuminate the positive change that is happening in finance, and to share stories from within it. So much good and inspiring news is buried in technical facts and figures. We often forget the human exchange of value that can exist at the heart of finance.

To share and spread stories of positive change, The Finance Innovation Lab started to document groundswells of innovation within the financial system that have bubbled up since the financial crisis in 2012. We did this by producing *Manifest*, a publication that interviews leaders from our community. It offers examples of alternative currencies, and local banking and products that counter financial exclusion.

This publication has been most popular among our mainstream community from the financial services sector, who had little idea about what was emerging on the fringes. In that way we are contributing to a new narrative within the financial system, although measuring this impact is challenging.

We've realized over time that one of most inspiring way of capturing these somewhat intangible insights and trends was through storytelling. As a team, we participated in a storytelling training, and have begun to embed it as a practice in all we do.

For example, we host an open-mic storytelling night at our monthly Lab drinks events, to which our broader community is invited. Ex-bankers and accountants and activist stand up in a pub in the city of London and quietly tell their personal stories regarding breakdown in the system, how they shifted careers, or the struggles they've faced as whistleblowers.

The connection created between strangers at these events is inspiring. Personal stories are always interesting, and they allow you to see more of the person in front of you, whoever they are. Plus, any truth or data contained within these stories is more fully received because of the attention and interest drawn by the personal element.

Finding new ways to track impact

We're all experimenting with ways to keep track of our impact. For example, Education Pioneers developed a storytelling methodology to track and trace what really matters to participants, and to help us identify what really supports them.

Instead of delivering long, dry evaluation and measurement impact reports, we offer a storytelling type of evaluation that's based on generating, sharing and using innovators' stories of their word on the ground. And in this process, we tend toward anticipating the future, rather than assessing results in terms of the past.

By doing this, we don't "affix" the evaluation parameters of our projects. Instead, we put the evaluation where the action is: in the innovator's interactions with peers or community—including the school, pupils, colleagues, parents, and school directors. The community is where most of the feedback and learning take place.

In practice, we construct feedback loops between innovators (teachers), their innovation communities (people who are affected by the positive or negative outcomes of an innovation—pupils, parents and school directors) and the support structure (a school policy, a government policy, or a program like Education Pioneers).

In feedback loops between these parties, we are especially looking for positive feedback, which helps teachers act and move forward (generating further feedback). We've coined this type of feedback "feed forward." Feed forward stories stimulate innovative behavior, and tend to point toward next steps without prescribing too rigidly. They allow for diversity and showcase a variety of voices, experiences and knowledges. These different perspectives are indispensable ingredients for innovation.

Our evaluation approach has proven to be of value for both the project manager and the teachers. But challenges remain. This type of evaluation is time-consuming. And many funders and more traditional researchers don't accept this methodology and its results as a legitimate way to measure and evaluate impact. Many still prefer "evidence-based" reports from experts connected to established academic research centers.

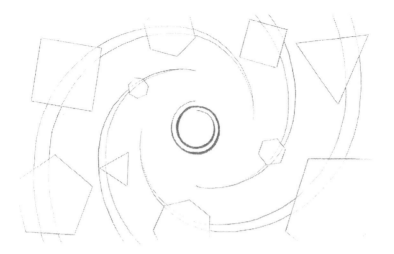

STAYING NIMBLE

O ur labs each occupy a specific position in between the old and the new, between massive challenges and emerging alternatives. These alternatives are sometimes small, sometimes even seemingly irrelevant, yet are impossible to ignore, especially in the long term.

Stuck systems produce various kinds of urgencies, and one of the most prominent ones is the constant impulse to grow. Discussions in the skyscraper world often sound like this: "You've supported 40 teachers, so let's now support 80, 160, until we've reached them all."

And that's completely understandable—after all, we're trying to make big changes in the world. The key challenge here is to find a way to grow our impact without becoming the same rigid system we're trying to transform. Can we work at scale and still be nimble? Or does scale imply compromise?

What our labs seem to have in common is a search to find news ways of spreading, replicating and diffusing. At La 27e Région, we help other people to create labs on their own. We open-source our processes so others can use them, build on them, adjust them to their own contexts, and drastically improve them.

The Finance Innovation Lab spins off projects into semi-autonomous units while maintaining oversight of their strategic direction. AuditFutures and Campaign Lab have both been seeded by the Finance Lab in partnership with external organizations, and now operate as part of its ecosystem.

At eLab, our 35 core members have been wrestling with the question of how to scale ideas and solutions. We recognize that the work we're doing is building an important foundation, but ultimately isn't sufficient in the face of a dwindling timeframe in which to address climate change and other important issues.

The temptation would be to continue replicating projects and expanding the core team. But eLab is working to move beyond mere replication. Instead, we're developing new elements of our "ecosystem" that provide scale in different ways—enabling us to connect with hundreds or thousands of stakeholders and decisionmakers while still maintaining our ability to be agile and innovate.

Most recently we launched eLab Accelerator as a way to catalyze the work of many other change agents and projects across the U.S. Our Accelerator convened 12 teams—more than 100 people who were already working to transform the electricity system—for a week-long intensive innovation workshop.

Through a facilitated process, learning from each other, and access to eLab expert faculty, these teams found that they could advance their projects significantly further than they would have on their own.

Coming out of eLab Accelerator, several teams have already made important independent progress that eLab will continue to support. For example, one team that included a utility partner, two leading global technology companies, a state regulator, and an environmental advocate is continuing to collaborate on a creative new pricing structure that better empowers customers.

In addition to following these teams from the inaugural Accelerator, eLab now plans to make Accelerator an annual event, and is actively adding elements to the eLab ecosystem. These elements include new approaches to working with specific industry segments, additional staff from our member organizations, and best practices across the industry.

At the InSTEDD iLabs we are in a catalyst position. Our iLabs take scalability as a human-centered design challenge right from the start.

We purposely *don't* staff for large-scale field support, because that would remove the incentive to run projects in a way that doesn't require constant handholding. When we create pilot programs, we test the main idea— for example, that same-day malaria reports can better direct resources and help reduce and eliminate the disease. But we also test scalability concepts. We ask the question "how will this go from 10 to 100 to 10,000 villages?"

If we run into issues that increase training costs or get in the way of field workers learning by themselves, we go back to the drawing board and address them in the tool design. For example, if one village health care worker can successfully train another one to use the tool, we can cut most of the operational expense of the project. If they can't train each other in this way, we redesign the tools until they can.

Unfortunately, many NGOs have a business model based on long-term support, which means that efficient scale is dis-incentivized in their funding. This creates a big cultural mismatch for projects up front.

At InSTEDD we work on global projects, and the iLabs are a core part of our scaling strategy. When iLabs and business development units are staffed and led by locals, who choose projects autonomously, each one can evolve, grow, shrink, hire, and shut down on their own terms and criteria.

Some people imagine it's about replication, but for us, scaling labs is more about local creation. We step back from local iLabs once they demonstrate strong local leadership with specific values, and they're meeting our criteria for social impact, financial sustainability and capacity building.

We don't try to impose any single recipe, structure or management style, and although we do have patterns and proven practices, we prefer leaders who are change agents themselves and will own and develop their own plans based on their own criteria.

At La 27e Région, we are currently right in the middle of this dilemma of scale and nimbleness. Our newest program, Re•acteur Public, has been designed as a vehicle to take the methods, processes, and thinking we've developed during the past six years and scale them in collaboration with a handful of regional councils.

On May 13th, 2014, about 100 people gathered to celebrate and join what is planned to be a four-year program led by a large consortium of public institutions. This group included a minister, some local officials, high-ranking public managers, and a group of social entrepreneurs and designers.

What does that mean for us as a lab? We haven't figured it out yet, but we're quite convinced that this new project will radically change the way we act and intervene. Certainly, if we want to create systemic change at the macro level, we need to broaden our scale of intervention; four or five regions isn't enough.

But how do we change the whole system, from the smallest city council to national state administration, without losing our edge? How do we make sure those big players are coming along for good reasons and not just to "labwash" their actions?

At Education Pioneers, we've grown from supporting 10 primary-school teachers in 2008 to a program supporting 45 teachers and 20 school leaders in primary, secondary and vocational schools in the Netherlands. EP has grown because the small pilots were successful and attracted media attention. This created momentum, which helped us to create demand and investment from larger, more established organizations.

There are consequences and challenges connected to growing our program. First of all, our project management is increasing. We need to manage more facilitation and infrastructure, financial resources and communication. We're also spending much more time on the phone, in meeting rooms, in front of the computer, and traveling.

A direct consequence of all this is that we have less time in the schools, where we meet teachers, pupils, and parents and listen to their needs. That's requiring us to find new ways of understanding what's going on with our projects and what's needed. We need to stay true to our core values, and we find personal contact and practice with teachers extremely important.

We've started to address this by creating an in-between structure of appointed coaches, who are in touch with the teachers and who manage the relationships with and between the teachers. The relationship management works well, but we still struggle to learn where the needs of the teachers lie. Due to lack of time and resources, we can't meet with the coaches as often as we'd like to hear their stories and ask for feedback to improve the infrastructure of the EP program.

So we still struggle to maintain the level of quality that's so important to us, and to keep our feedback loops in place—so that we're not merely delivering a blue-printed program according to what we think teachers need.

We're currently thinking that Education Pioneers shouldn't grow larger itself, but instead focus on how we could embed more innovative, teacher-initiated practices structurally into school policies and organizations.

It remains questionable whether experimentation from the inside out can really contribute to the emergence of a system that better accommodates the needs of students, nor is it clear whether more experimental space for teachers can alter the national education system at large.

In the end, teachers are still confined in the same systemic structure, and we aren't actually challenging the concept of education itself, or the concept of having teachers as a whole. There are still schools, classrooms, educational material, required classes, teachers, and students, with a national inspection service and national education policies.

Currently, our programs don't question the assumption that schools present the best educational format to accommodate students in our 21st century. If we think our future needs a different type of education, then might the next step be to create a movement that challenges the educational field to "un-school?"

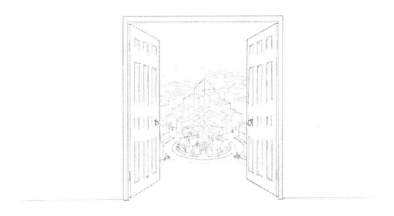

AN INVITATION

W e came to this process with a multitude of agendas and perspectives. Most of us hadn't met or worked together before. Yet as the first chapter reveals, we rapidly found common ground. We agreed that we're living in interesting, exciting and challenging times—times of fundamental transition in the way we organize our societies, our economies and the relations between people and planet. And this transition demands that we start paying attention to new ways of generating and disseminating knowledge.

Can we really understand and describe the new emerging world with the knowledge frameworks of the old? Can we find ways to conceptualize and theorize about a fast-emerging wave of experimental places for systemic change in real time?

This is an important question, because we believe that there's an abundance of energy, ideas, and untapped potential that we can leverage to address big challenges—if only we can find ways to connect and learn faster, better, deeper.

In finishing this book, we've come to the end of an experiment in networked knowledge production, rooted in the everyday practices and struggle of the world in our labs. We spent four days moving between the theoretical underpinnings and the day-to-day experience of our work; between collaboration, consultation, and consensus-building and the desire to represent the truth of our authentic individual experiences.

Teams formed and reformed. We listened and hypothesized; we prototyped and iterated (and iterated again); we disagreed and found common ground.

Come to think of it, our experience looked and felt a lot like a lab. This book rose from the rubble. From questioning ownership and authorship, a willingness arose to forego ownership of ideas in order to represent a multitude of voices and contributions.

This demonstrates what we can do when we join forces in innovative and experimental ways to address social challenges. It reveals what's possible when you apply these "lab" processes to a learning experience, embracing new ways of working and a transformative learning experience.

We were tempted to clean up a few of the paradoxes, questions, and ambiguities that emerged in our dialogue and discussion, but decided not to. In the "old" world, books are end-products, little skyscrapers in themselves. In this book, part of the point was to bring in elements of the spaces in between—to embody in real time that which we were expressing and describing.

If you're one of those people also working on systemic change, within or outside of the lab world, we hope that this book will encourage you to push on. Don't let yourself be held back by complexities and frustrations.

We also hope this book conveys something of an invitation for an emerging community of practice around labs—and, more broadly, an invitation to create spaces and projects for systemic change everywhere.

Share your feedback, distribute the book, host events, and prototype with the insights from this book.

In a world of skyscrapers and sidewalks, we have sought to illuminate the space in between, and we will continue to do so. Whichever part of the landscape you find yourself in, we invite you to step into that space.

AKNOWLEDGEMENTS

This collaborative book would not have been possible without the support of many. First and foremost, we acknowledge the contributing authors from the labs listed below. We thank our funders Hivos in the Netherlands and the Economic and Social Research Council (ESRC) in the United Kingdom. Without invaluable in-kind support provided by Natural Innovation team, this book wouldn't have come into existence. We also want to thank the Innovation Knowledge and Organisational Networks (IKON) research group at the Warwick Business School for supporting the workshop and Book Sprint that made this book possible.

Appreciation also for our friends at iceCairo, a colleague lab in Egypt, where the original idea for this Book Sprint was born during a conversation between Hendrik Tiesinga and Adam Hyde at their "eco-cities camp" in early 2013. The project received a second important boost during Kennisland & Hivos' "Lab2: A Lab on Labs" workshop, facilitating further crucial connections between the conveners of this book.

This book is a living example of how unintended positive spin-offs are generated by the creative encounters that happen in social labs around the world.

ABOUT THE AUTHORS

Remko Berkhout works as a consultant and associate advisor for Hivos on strategy and innovation. He holds a Master of Science degree in Sociological Economics from the University of Rotterdam and spent the last 15 years supporting capacity and strategy development with NGOs in India, Bangladesh and Mozambique.

From 2009 to 2013, Remko worked with Hivos to lead knowledge initiatives that facilitated research and dialogue among activists, practitioners, and policymakers regarding the fast-changing nature and manifestation of civic action around the world. In that capacity, Remko has also been exploring alternative forms of knowledge production, including experiments with participatory action research, immersive learning, and alternative publication formats. Recently he's been exploring the fertile middle ground between social innovation and international development to find and analyze new strategies for systemic change.

Lena Hansen is a Principal with Rocky Mountain Institute's electricity practice, where she's co-led the Electricity Innovation Lab (eLab) since its inception in 2012. Lena coauthored the electricity chapter of RMI's 2011 book *Reinventing Fire: Bold Business Solutions for a New Energy Era*. This book led

Lena and her colleagues to look for new approaches to accelerating change in the very-slow-to-change, risk-averse U.S. electricity system, which is now facing disruptive challenges and opportunities.

Lena holds a Master's degree in environmental economics and policy from Duke University, and a Bachelor's degree in physics with astronomy from the University of North Carolina-Chapel Hill.

Josh Harvey leads the United Nation Children's Fund (UNICEF) Innovations Lab Kosovo, a unit of UNICEF Kosovo* Programme and part of a collective of innovation peeps throughout UNICEF and across the globe looking (with humility) at how to reimagine UNICEF for a changed world.

Josh is particularly interested in how human-centered design and co-creative practices overlap with a rights-based approach. He's also interested in rethinking the private sector's relationship with social good, and in how incubation and acceleration models can be repurposed to advance empowerment and participation.

Josh holds a Master's degree in International Development and Education from Columbia University Graduate School of Education (Teachers College), and he is a former Teach for America corps member (Newark '06).

Eduardo Jezierski is the CEO of InSTEDD (http://instedd. org), which includes global oversight of the iLabs. He has built a career bridging systemic gaps in how technology is applied to pressing challenges. This included large-scale enterprise computing and collaboration challenges at Microsoft, and then shifted full-time to "technology with purpose" work when he joined InSTEDD.

Making social impact technology real has required transcending organizational, company, and sector silos; building passionate teams of entrepreneurs and intrapreneurs; and applying context-appropriate, iterative, agile, and exploratory approaches to help build a better society.

While authoring this book, Ed consulted with and tried to channel the voices of Channe Suy and Nicolás di Tada, who lead the InSTEDD iLabs in Southeast Asia and Latin America.

Marlieke Kieboom is a researcher and advisor with Kennisland. The question she's most passionate about and focused on is "how can we make knowledge useful to support people's innovative practices?"

To wrestle with this question, she designs new learning infrastructures (like Lab2: A Lab of Labs) and research methodologies (such as dynamic evaluation), and she writes avidly about the challenges in her work (as in her latest paper, "Lab Matters").

Marlieke obtained a Master of Science degree in Anthropology (Utrecht University, NL) and Master of Arts in Conflict and Governance (Simon Fraser University, CA). Her thematic expertise lies somewhere between education, governance, politics, and cheese making.

Magali Marlin is the project manager in charge of La 27e Région's development. Exploring the cracks and edges of public policymaking to find ways to make it more human-centred, resilient, and efficient is what gets her on the field every day. She decided to step into La 27e Région in March 2012, puzzled by its obscure yet intriguing project of transforming local public policies with the help of design.

Today, her job consists of coordinating various program teams at La 27e Région, and helping to set the stage for the next program to be deployed nationwide. Magali's background is in social sciences (sociology, politics). She holds a Master of Science degree in Urban and Territorial Strategies (Sciences Po Paris).

Kimon Moerbeek is co-founder of Education Pioneers. He is an advisor at Kennisland and has been involved in a range of projects to foster change and social innovation, mostly in the education field. His main focus is how people can initiate positive development in an organizational context to get more out of their own and each other's potential. Kimon holds a Research Master in Social Sciences (University of Amsterdam).

Anna Lochard is a researcher with La 27e Région. Her everyday challenge is connecting researchers and labs from all over the world with the most exciting things that are happening in French administrations—partly thanks to La 27e Région's action. The aim of building these bridges is to develop research action programs and create open-source and actionable knowledge. She holds Master's degree in Management Sciences from the Mines ParisTech Engineering School, a Master's degree in Urban Planning from the Ecole Nationale des Ponts et Chaussées, and a specialization in dumpster diving.

Rachel Sinha is Sustainability Manager of The Institute of Chartered Accountants in England and Wales, and co-founder of The Finance Innovation Lab. For her work in the lab, she was named Management Today and BSkyB's Future Leader of Sustainability, and invited to be a member of the European Commission Expert Group on Social Business.

She is one of The Point People who created the website systemschangers.com, designed to shine a light on the work of systems-change practitioners in the UK. She also helped to convene the "Leaders Shaping Market Systems" project with The Criterion Institute in the US.

Rachel has a Bachelor's degree in Psychology and a Master's degree in Marketing, and was a scholar at THNK, the Amsterdam School of Creative Leadership.

Mariko Takeuchi is the founding Director of inCompass Human-Centered Innovation Lab (hyperlinkwww.incompass. org) at iDE (ideorg.org). She has spent the last 10 years using a human-centered approach to designing solutions for humans that resonate deeply with them.

She initially began designing for the world's wealthiest populations, on behalf of multinationals such as Unilever and in a range of industries including beer, publishing, financial planning, chocolate, confectionary, and weddings. During the last four years, she has been working and living within the developing world to design equally innovative solutions that delight and improve the lives of the world's poorest populations.

Mariko is a passionate advocate for treating the poor as paying customers, and can talk for hours (if given the chance) about why a human-centered approach is critical to designing sustainable solutions for the developing world.

Hendrik Tiesinga is a curator, designer, and facilitator of multi-stakeholder innovation labs and networks. He is a co-founder of Natural Innovation, a social innovation agency. He is the editor, curator, and producer of the *Labcraft* book.

Hendrik was also a co-founder of the Finance Innovation Lab in London, convened in 2008 by WWF-UK and the Institute of Chartered Accountants. He has designed and facilitated complex multi-stakeholder projects across Europe, North America, and the Arab world, working with organizations and networks ranging from grassroots social entrepreneurs and artists to the European Commission, the Big 4 Audit Firms, Proctor & Gamble, and Siemens.

Hendrik is also a doctoral researcher at Warwick Business School in the UK, and currently a visiting scholar at UC Berkeley. His research focuses on the practices and impacts of innovation labs in addressing complex societal challenges.

ABOUT NATURAL INNOVATION

Natural Innovation is a network of collaborators based in Europe, Africa, and the Americas. As a social enterprise, we specialize in incubating and facilitating multi-stakeholder innovation labs and networks. We partner with governments, businesses, multilateral institutions and civil-society organizations to develop strategies that cultivate thriving innovation eco-systems.

Inspired by nature, we're convinced that real innovation arises in the creative tension that exists between different elements of a social ecology. Our work is to cultivate the right conditions for these diverse groups of people to come together and co-create meaningful solutions.

Natural Innovation has extensive experience in curating and facilitating collaborative innovation in a wide range of arenas including finance, food, energy, social enterprise, sustainability, international development, academia, and democracy development.

Visit our website at www.natural-innovation.net

ABOUT THE HIVOS CIVIC EXPLORATIONS PROGRAM

The idea of a Book Sprint on the practices of social labs was supported by the Hivos Civic Explorations program. This program works with academics, development practitioners, and activists around the world to make sense of the changing face of civic action (more info at www.hivos.org/knowledge-programme). It engages in action research, dialogue, and experiments related to methodology. All of these strands were woven into this project.

Social labs are a fast-growing phenomenon around the world and merit critical attention. After participating in several global knowledge events through labs, the Hivos Civic Explorations program realized that more attention needed to be paid to the everyday practices of labs and the substance of their work. The Book Sprint method seemed to suit the rhythms and priorities of lab practitioners: eager to share and learn, interested in open ways of knowledge production, time-strapped and action-oriented.

ABOUT BOOK SPRINTS

A Book Sprint brings together a group to produce a book in three to five days. There is no pre-production, and a facilitator guides the group from zero to creating a book. The books produced are high-quality content, and can be made available immediately at the end of the sprint via print-on-demand services and eBook formats. For more information, please see http://www.booksprints.net. Adam Hyde, the founder of the Book Sprint methodology, facilitated this Book Sprint.

| LABCRAFT

JOIN THE LABCRAFT COMMUNITY

The creation of Labcraft was truly a communal effort of different innovation labs and authors coming together. We invite you to become part of this growing Labcraft community. You can do this by joining our Facebook or Linkedin group. This way you'll stay up to date with the latest development of the labs features in this book as well as many more. You stay up to date by joining our newsletter on our www.labcraft.co website.

And if you are part of a social innovation lab yourself, put it on map! You can do this on the Lapmap on our website.

We really hope you enjoyed reading our book. You can help us spread the word by writing mini-review on Facebook, Twitter or your blog with a link to www.labcraf.co or #labcraft. You can do the same on our Amazon book page.

Feel free to drop us a message on our website

www.labcraft.co if you have any questions or suggestions.

- The Labcraft Team

Lightning Source UK Ltd.
Milton Keynes UK
UKOW02f1322160215

246349UK00003BA/256/P

9 780990 592709